DATE DUE	
AUG 0 2 1986	
JAN 0 3 1987	
DEC 18 1992	
12 02 92	
05. 7. 93	
BRODART, INC	Cat. No. 23-221

THE LANGUAGE OF GESTURE

THE LANGUAGE OF GESTURE

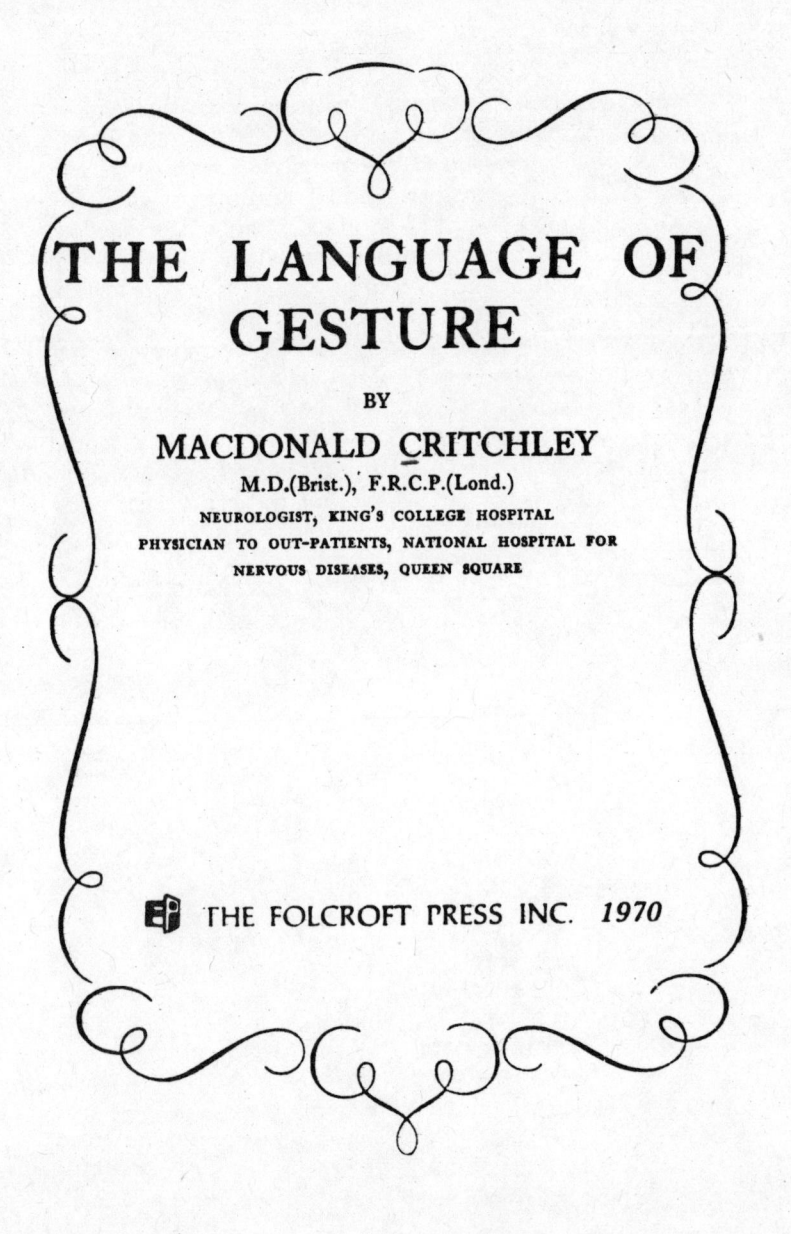

BY

MACDONALD CRITCHLEY
M.D.(Brist.), F.R.C.P.(Lond.)
NEUROLOGIST, KING'S COLLEGE HOSPITAL
PHYSICIAN TO OUT-PATIENTS, NATIONAL HOSPITAL FOR
NERVOUS DISEASES, QUEEN SQUARE

THE FOLCROFT PRESS INC. 1970

THE LANGUAGE OF GESTURE

BY

MACDONALD CRITCHLEY

M.D.(Brist.), F.R.C.P.(Lond.)

NEUROLOGIST, KING'S COLLEGE HOSPITAL
PHYSICIAN TO OUT-PATIENTS, NATIONAL HOSPITAL FOR
NERVOUS DISEASES, QUEEN SQUARE

LONDON
EDWARD ARNOLD & CO.

FIRST PUBLISHED 1939
All rights reserved

PRINTED IN GREAT BRITAIN BY
JARROLD AND SONS LTD. NORWICH

PREFACE

IF, as Disraeli asserted, "nine-tenths of the existing books are nonsense," some explanation is obviously required for adding to the sum-total of confusion. Goethe, who himself was not guiltless in this connection, described writing as the product of a "busy idleness," and this indeed has been the author's sole excuse for so amusing himself. The study of gesture has constituted an interesting and perhaps not altogether an unpractical by-product of the broader problem of speech in general.

Interest in this matter was originally aroused a few years ago when a deaf-mute patient presented himself at the National Hospital, Queen Square, on account of the effects of a mild stroke. This man had sustained a small vascular lesion within the left cerebral hemisphere; an incomplete and evanescent right-sided paralysis had supervened and passed, but there had remained a defect in the powers of expression by way of his accustomed sign-talk. In other words, there had arisen a virtual "aphasia" in a mute subject, in whom finger-talk had for years ousted verbalization from speech. Study of this case, unique in medical records, led to an inquiry into the methods whereby deaf-mutes communicated their wishes and ideas to each other. One came to realize that there exists among the deaf and dumb a gestural system of speech which is independent of racial and linguistic barriers and which is largely instinctive in its nature. A striking similarity was found between this system of gestures, and the sign-talk practised by certain aboriginal communities.

These observations, in no way original, were nevertheless unfamiliar within medical circles, despite their very great importance. Here was an aspect of language which was in some ways older and more primitive than spoken speech. The functions of gesture; its role as an embellishment of articulate speech and as a substitute; its place among expressive movements in general, were some of the problems which led to this present publication.

M. C.

June 1939

CONTENTS

CHAPTER		PAGE
I.	GESTURE AND EXPRESSIVE MOVEMENTS	9
II.	GESTURE AND SPEECH, FROM THE STANDPOINT OF PHILOLOGY AND PHONETICS	15
III.	THE NEUROLOGY OF GESTURE	25
IV.	THE SIGN-TALK OF DEAF-MUTES	32
V.	SIGN-LANGUAGE AMONG THE NORTH-AMERICAN INDIANS	42
VI.	SIGN-TALK AMONG AUSTRALIAN ABORIGINES	46
VII.	SIGN-LANGUAGE IN RELIGIOUS COMMUNITIES	51
VIII.	SIGN-LANGUAGE: SECRET SOCIETIES	54
IX.	SIGN-LANGUAGE IN ORIENTAL LITERATURE	59
X.	INDIAN MYTHOLOGY	65
XI.	OCCUPATIONAL SIGN-LANGUAGES; DIGITAL METHODS OF COUNTING	73
XII.	SIGN-LANGUAGE AND SYMBOLISM	78
XIII.	GESTURE IN CONVERSATION: THE NEAPOLITANS AND THE LEVANTINES	85
XIV.	THE ART OF RHETORIC	94
XV.	THE ART OF MIMING AND THE DANCE	98
XVI.	THE GRAECO-ROMAN THEATRE	104
XVII.	THE ORIENTAL THEATRE	110
XVIII.	GESTURE AS A PRECURSOR OF SPEECH	116
	INDEX	125

CHAPTER I
GESTURE AND EXPRESSIVE MOVEMENTS

ALTHOUGH the usual conception of "speech" is the employment of articulate utterance, to the biologist something much wider is implied. The latter would define human speech as the ability not only to make known one's feelings and ideas, but also to recognize the feelings and ideas of another; the means by which this inter-communication is effected includes, in addition to vocal and audible articulatory sound, writing, drawing, gesture, and even certain art-forms such as music, painting, sculpture and the dance.

This broader definition of speech is justified when one recalls the plight of a man finding himself in a foreign country where the language is unfamiliar. In such circumstances, all the extraneous non-vocal forms of speech will be needed in order to make contact with his entourage.

It should be realized, furthermore, that gesture is not only one of the important means whereby ideas and emotions are declared and recognized, but that it also serves as an important adjuvant to spoken speech. Thus gesture, gesticulation and facial movements of expression usually accompany the act of talking, and serve to emphasize the content of what is said. To quote the words of Lhermitte[1] ... "du discours oral qu'il suit, comme l'ombre suit le corps, ce langage par les gestes reflète mille nuances qui

[1] Lhermitte, J., *L'Encephale*, 1938, *33* (*i*), 1.

sans lui nous echapperaient et en traduit l'inexprimé."
The extent to which gesticulation accompanies spoken speech varies widely, depending upon circumstances, as well as upon personal and racial factors.

Evidence collected from developmental and comparative philology, goes deeper, by suggesting that gestures may constitute an important aspect of speech with origins perhaps more remote than verbalization. In this way gestures or sign-talk may represent a forerunner, or one of the forerunners, of human speech.

But gesture has done more than serve as a kind of parent, which having engendered spoken speech, continues to live and expand in the company of its offspring. Gesture has also developed along lines of its own. Thus, we can trace elaborations of gesture which have more or less broken away from spoken speech, in various circumstances:

> (1) It has evolved its own particular art-form, namely, the cult of miming, pantomime and the dance.
> (2) Gestures have become incorporated within the more esoteric aspects of religion, to form an elaborate ritual of symbolology.
> (3) In like manner, certain gestures have been curtailed, stylized, abbreviated and later they have passed into the common currency of ordinary usage. In this way have arisen such conventional gestures as the military salute, the handshake and the kiss.
> (4) For very diverse reasons, systems of sign-language have evolved and may be utilized to the total exclusion of spoken speech.

Before undertaking a study of gesture as a component of speech, it is necessary to be clear as to the precise meaning of our terminology. Unfortunately the words "gesture," "gesticulation," "miming," "mimic movements," "pantomime," are employed in rather a haphazard fashion. It would be better to restrict the word "pantomime" to that variety of dumb-show which aims at expressing an idea, while "gesture" or its diminutive "gesticulation" should be made to connote those movements, particularly of the hands and face, which accompany speech for the purpose of emphasis. Pantomime is silent acting, while gesture is merely a kind of italicized speech. To employ the terminology of Hughlings Jackson we may compare the relationship of pantomime to gesture, with that of propositionizing to emotional utterance. It must be borne in mind, however, that no very sharp frontier separates gesture from pantomime, and that at times expressive movements cannot readily be assigned to one or the other category. The same action can serve in either capacity.

The term "physiognomy" primarily and literally refers to the art of divining character by a study of the face. It can also be expanded so as to apply to those grimacing movements of the face which accompany the play of the emotions and which—though capable of being controlled by willed efforts—are in the main involuntary or quasi-deliberate. One may also include within the compass of this term, those cutaneous phenomena of a primitive and protective nature, subserved by the autonomic nervous system and which are almost entirely outside the control of volition; the manifestation of blushing, pallor, horripilation, goose-flesh and sweating belong here. Tremor of the hands, dryness of the mouth, increase or decrease in the muscular tonus, alteration in stance and attitude, are also to be regarded as expressive movements of a more automatic and less voluntary character.

We know, primarily from the studies of Darwin, that emotional movements, particularly those of physiognomy, represent a very primitive and widely diffused phenomenon. Not only are these movements so consistent in character as to be readily recognized by all mankind, whatever the language, culture, civilization and education, but they are demonstrable in typical guise in persons who from birth have been devoid of sight. Furthermore, the same emotional movements can be witnessed among the animal kingdom in a small range of cruder manifestations of more obvious utilitarian significance.[1]

Pantomimic movements are obviously of much later development and are found only in the human race. Their appearance usually denotes a variant of propositionizing, though in some cases the form of the mimicry may be distorted, so that the ultimate significance is obscured. Thus the raising of the hand to the forehead—which now constitutes a military salute—was originally a way of demonstrating that the hand held no offensive weapon.

[1] A detailed account of the contributions to this subject made by Descartes, Lebrun (the painter), the natural historian Buffon, Cuyer, Campes, Sir Charles Bell, Spencer, Wundt, Cannon and others, is contained in the monographs of G. Dumas, *Nouveau traité de psychologie*. Tome iii. Fascic. 2 and 3. Paris. Alcan. 1937.

GESTURE AND EXPRESSIVE MOVEMENTS 13

The employment of pantomime and gesture is not an essential part of human conduct or speech, though it must be extremely rare for all traces of expressive movement to be excluded. Even in the severest bradykinetic-hypertonic syndromes of extrapyramidal disease, such as Parkinsonism, some attenuated vestiges may still be traced. The abundance of both gesture and pantomime usually increases directly with the degree of volubility, and racial characteristics are important in this connection. One recalls the wealth of emotional movement displayed by the Latins, the Kelts and some Oriental races, in contrast to the poise and relative immobility of Nordic peoples. The influence of tradition and training must not be overlooked in this respect, however, particularly when one encounters gestures which contradict our conventional usages.

Recent studies among American immigrants have indeed suggested that cultural factors are far more important than racial ones in the development of gesture.

The extent and pattern of expressive movements are commonly regarded as an individual peculiarity, as much a part of the subject as physical build, mode of speech, handwriting, gait, choice of apparel, and character. All these manifestations of total personality are sometimes included within the term "psychomotorik." This study, according to the Russian child-psychologist Oseretsky, embraces three subdivisions: (1) *motometric*, or the measurement of expressive movements; (2) *motographic*, or the methods of recording them; and (3) *motoscopic*, or the description and analysis of such movements (posture, pose, facial expression, gesticulation, handshake, gait, speech, handwriting, automatic movements, pathological movements). That the idea of a correlation between personality and mimetic characteristics is a true one, capable of experimental proof, seems to be borne out by the work of Allport and Vernon.[1] These authors also quote Ruttman's suggestion that with advancing years there is a greater uniformity between manual and verbal expressive activities, and a closer correspondence between them and personality-traits. Hand-movements and speech lose their standardized features of immaturity and evolve along with the progressive integration of the individual. "The pedant becomes more and more pedantic in speech and gesture; the soldier, more and more soldierly."

[1] Allport, G. W., and Vernon, P. E., *Studies in Expressive Movements*. New York. 1933.

CHAPTER II

GESTURE AND SPEECH, FROM THE STANDPOINT OF PHILOLOGY AND PHONETICS

The function of gesture in speech is, as already mentioned, important. Closer scrutiny shows that its role may be—if not fundamental—at least of profound etymological significance.

Discussion of this relationship centres around the problem of language; its origins; and in particular the so-called "natural" theories which trace intimate connections between the sound of a word and its meaning (Plato; Diodorus; Lucretius;[1] de Brosses;[2] Wedgwood[3]). For centuries, philologists and philosophers have devoted considerable thought to this question, though exaggeration and mutual recrimination have done much to discredit the sound work which has been carried out. Those who subscribe to a remote but "natural" origin of words are opposed by those who regard the faculty of speech with almost superstitious veneration, and, emulating the etymologists of Socrates, are content to ascribe the first words to the arbitrary choice of the gods. Unfortunately, the supporters of a "natural" origin of words cannot agree as to what constitutes the all-important link between sound and meaning; one is tempted to conclude that their theories are not mutually exclusive, but that they are capable of reconciliation.

[1] Lucretius, T., *De rerum natura*. Book I.
[2] De Brosses, C., *Traité de la formation mecanique des langues*. 1765.
[3] Wedgwood, H., *Origin of Language*. 1866.

Two of the hypotheses assume an imitative origin of speech-sounds. Thus we have, what have been flippantly termed by Max Müller, the "bow-wow" and the "ding-dong" hypotheses (Herder). The former seeks to trace the origin of words to the mimicry of animal cries, and the latter to the imitation of other noises. Both these processes are traceable in the onomatopoea (or echoism) of grammarians, where the sound of the words suggests the noise of the function or qualities of the object named. Thus we have names of animals derived from their cries or calls; e.g. the Australian *twonk* "frog"; the Chinese *maou* "cat"; the Sanskrit *kâka* "crow"; the Latin *pipio* "pigeon"; the Greek *boûs* "ox"; and the English *cuckoo, whip-poor-will, peewit*. In the same way we instance the terms *hum, buzz, chirp, squeak, purr, twitter*. Secondly, there are words expressing audible human activities. Tylor[1] has given many striking examples taken from a diversity of primitive languages. He mentions the forms *pu, puf, bu, buf, fu, fuf*, signifying "blowing" or "puffing," e.g. Malay *puput*; Tongan *buhi*; Maori *pupui*; Australian *bwa-bun*; Galla *bufa*; Zulu *futa*; Quiché *puba*; Tupi *ypeû*; Finnish *puhkia*; Hebrew *puach*; Danish *puste*; Lithuanian *púciu*; and so on throughout many other languages. A musket or rifle was given the name *pu* from the sound of the report heard at a distance coupled with the sight of the "puff" of smoke. In South Africa they speak of *umpu*; in North America they say "to make *poo*" for "to shoot." The colloquial German word for pistol

---

[1] Tylor, E. B., *Primitive Culture*. 2 vols. London. 1873.

PHILOLOGY AND PHONETICS 17

is *Puffer*. Analogy with the verb "to blow" gives us the blow-tube called in Yucatan a *pub*, in South America a *pucuna* and by the Comamas a *puna*. In the same way we can point to the Quichian *puhucuni* "to light a fire," *puyu* "a cloud"; Tupi *púpú* "to boil"; Galla *bube* "wind"; Kanuri *fungin* "to blow," and *bubute* "bellows"; Zulu *fu* "a cloud," *futo* "bellows"; *fumfu* "blown about like grass in a wind"; and *fumfuta* "confused."

Other groups of imitative words can be discovered in those made with closed lips to denote "*mum*" or "*mumble*." Thus Tylor[1] has collected from primitive languages such examples as: Vei *mu mu* "dumb"; Mpongwe *imamu* "dumb"; Zulu *mumatu* "to close the lips," and *mumutu* "to eat mouthfuls"; Tahitian *mamu* "to be silent"; Fijian *nomo nomo*; Quiché *mem* "mute"; Quichua *amu* "dumb." Then there are the imitative forms to indicate a "sneeze" (Sanskrit *Kshu*; Chilian *echiun*; Quichua *achhini*; Brazilian tribes *techa-ai*; *haitschu, atchian*, etc.) To denote food or eating we have the onomatopoeic words *njam* and *njam-njam* (Surinam); *g'nam-ang* (Australian); *nim-nim* (Susu); and the Zulu word *nambita* "to smack the lips after eating." Then too we have the Chinese word amongst children *nam* "eating" and the Swedish "*Namnam*" meaning a "titbit." In the Yakama tongue, the word "to love" used when referring to children or pet animals is *nem-no-sha* (= to make n'm-n'.)

But onomatopoeic words are not only directly imitative but they are—in many instances at least—

[1] Tylor, E. B., *Early History of Mankind*. 3rd edition. London. 1878.

2

"mimic," that is to say, they represent audible gestures of an imitative sort. This aspect of etymology cannot account for more than a fraction of the words in use. Years ago Max Müller[1] poured scorn upon the theory of onomatopoeia as a basis of language. . . . "The number of names which are really formed by an imitation of sound dwindle down to a very small quotum, if cross-examined by the comparative philologist; and we are left in the end with the conviction that though *a* language might have been made out of the roaring, fizzing, hissing, gabbling, twittering, cracking, banging, slamming and rattling sounds of nature, the tongues with which we are acquainted point to a different origin."

Other adherents of the natural origin of language believe with Horne Tooke that words are derived from common interjectional utterances, i.e. the "poohpooh" theory as it was dubbed by Max Müller.

An example given by de Brosses and quoted by Tylor will serve in illustration. The Latin word *stare* "to stand" originates, it is claimed, in an expressive sound; the *st!* representing an interjection of arrest—stop! or stand still! The same sound is employed to enjoin silence, as in the English *whist!* or *hist!* the Welsh *ust!* the French *chut!* the Italian *zitto!* the Swedish *tyst!* the Russian *st!* A Latin line "Isis, et Harpocrates digito qui significat st!" can be quoted where the st! is comparable with the gesture of a finger on the lips.

If, as Tooke suggested, "the dominion of speech

---

[1] Müller, M., *Science of Language*, vol. 1, p. 419. London. 1877. (2 vols.)

is erected upon the downfall of interjections," we may affirm that vestiges of an exclamatory character, although demonstrable here and there in current speech, are found in only very scant traces. It must be remembered too that certain sounds now employed as interjections, are really broken-down sense-words (e.g. *hélas* (alas) from *lassus* (tired, miserable)). Their mere existence is of importance, however, for interjections are utterances of a strong emotional content, and—even more than onomatopoeic words—can be regarded as audible gestures. A sudden emotion, whether of disgust, fear, pain, joy or sorrow, produces not only visible expressive movements of the face and limbs, but similar though unseen movements of the articulatory muscles. The resulting exclamation is as much a gesture as the movements of the limbs or face.

In addition to these views of imitative and interjectional origins of speech (both of which imply the intervention of gesture), attempts have been made to trace an even deeper analogy between gesture and vocal speech. Some philologists and phoneticists, notably Jousse, Morlaas,[1] Jespersen,[2] Paget,[3,4] and Davis[5] have taught that all speech is an elaboration of phonated buccal-labio-lingual gestures. They, too, have attempted to trace in the English language especially, an intimate connection between the

---

[1] Morlaas, J., *L'Encéphale*, 1935, *30* (i), 197.
[2] Jespersen, O., *Language. Its nature, development and origin.* New York. 1922.
[3] Paget, Sir R., *This English*. London. 1935.
[4] Paget, Sir R., *Human Speech*. London. 1930.
[5] Davis, T. K., *Jour. Nerv. and Ment. Dis.* 1938, *88*, 491.

sound of a word and its meaning. Paget suggests that man originally expressed himself by gesture, and "as he gesticulated with his hands, his tongue, lips and jaw unconsciously followed suit in a ridiculous fashion, understudying the action of the hands." Later, movements of the jaws and mouth actually supplanted the manual gestures, when it was found that expiration of air through the oral cavities produced a wide range of audible mouth-gestures, or voiced speech.

This view approximates, of course, to yet another "natural" theory of the origin of language, namely, the "yo-heave-ho" hypothesis. Speech is regarded by the adherents as representing the outcome of man's muscular and physical exertions wherein the laryngeal musculature takes part.

Paget[1] gives many examples of parallelism between sound and meaning. Thus he believes that in English the vowel-sound *ah* refers to anything which is wide open, large, spacious, or flat; that "*i*" and "*ee*" refer to that which is high, forward-placed, or little (e.g. steeple, teeny, peak); and that "*aw*" connotes a cavity (e.g. yawn) and "*oo*" something enclosed, full, tubular, or elongated (e.g. room, tube, loop). In the same way, specific meanings are linked with various consonantal forms, e.g. "*s*" and "*z*" suggest something reaching forwards or upwards (e.g. send, steep, gaze, stare), "*l*" indicates motion to or from a point (e.g. length, long, leave) and "*sn*" anything pertaining to the nose (snort, snout, snuff, sneeze, etc.).

Other instances have been adduced. Thus the

[1] Paget, Sir R., *This English*. London. 1935.

combination "*fl-*" is said to suggest movement; usually up or inward (fly, flow, flop); "*cr-*" surrounding, containing, gripping, punching or bending (crumble, crush, crack, cram), "*sl-*" sliding back or down (slide, slip, slither, slump, slim, slight, slow, slur); "*-ump*" projecting, or inflated, or round (hump, bump, dump, rump, lump, trump), "*-m*" or "*-mb*" . . . enclosed (room, tomb); "*sh-*" . . . a high, thin surface or layer (shoot, shimmer, shore, shift, shirt, sheet, shin); "*st-*" drawn up, hold up, or contract (stand, still, stop, start, stem); "*str-*" extending from here to there (stretch, street, strand, stream).

In this way, according to Paget, an intimate alliance between the sound of a word and its meaning can be traced in about four-fifths of all short words in the English language. This principle also applies to other tongues. In contradistinction to the purely imitative process of onomatopoeia, Paget suggests the term "schematopoeia."

Similarly, Davis has recently insisted that speech began in and from action and that all first sounds were modes of behaviour and expressions of emotional tension. Davis, who seems to have been unaware of Paget's work, emphasizes the role of onomatopoeia, and quotes at length Jespersen's statements on sound symbolism. The last named believed that words expressive of movements, often begin with "*l-*" combinations: float, flow, flag, flake, flicker, flutter, flit, flurry, flirt, slide, slip, sleep, glide, ply. A short vowel suddenly interrupted by a stopped consonant may connote the sound produced by a sudden striking movement (pat, tap, knock). A natural connection is affirmed between high tones (sounds with very rapid vibrations) and light; and conversely, between low tones and darkness. The words gleam, glimmer, glitter are contrasted with gloom. Davis[1] would also add words which metaphorically relate to darkness or the dark side of things, e.g. murder, sombre, múrky, furtive, under; while the *u* sound is linked with words denoting a "dark" state of mind—glum, glumpy, grumpy, sulken, sullen, moody, dumps. Jespersen associates the same "dull" vowel-sounds with words for dislike, disgust or scorn: blunder, bungle, clumsy, humdrum, humbug, slum, slush, sloven, muck, mud, muddle, mug, numbskull, dunderhead.[2] Interesting remarks are made by Davis as to the tension of the muscles of the lip and face, as indicative of the mood in schizophrenic patients. The author suggests that primitive palatal (guttural) sounds were initially matched up with the emotions of intestinal, sexual and vital significance. "They helped to give away the 'guts' of that speaker." On the other hand, the labial sounds to a less degree partook of this intimacy with those parts of most intense living. Yerkes and Learned's work on chimpanzee talk is quoted in this connection. The *g* and *k* sounds—*gak, galk, gah, gha, ghak, gho, ghoo, gaha, kabkah, koko, kuku, kyah, knoh, kabhah, kabhah, kabhaha* are largely "food-words" and sounds associated with excitement.

---

[1] Davis, T. K., *loc. cit.*
[2] We are reminded here of a recent statement by O. St. J. Gogarty (*Tumbling in the Hay*. London. 1939) that most of the ominous words in the language are built about the vowel lowest in the scale, *u* (dung, numa, lump, turgescent, rum, slum).

Rothman and Teuber noted that chimpanzees uttered *oh* sounds in joyful exclamation, the height of the tone varying directly with the degree of excitement. Deep *u* sounds were used in states of grief.

Davis also mentions the properties of words dominated by the letter *v*. There is a quality of cleaving incisiveness and of strength; the edge of a wedge seems to be suggested (victory, victim, invincible, vile, vice, vigour, vivid, valour, vast, vengeance, venom, venus, verve, viscera, victim, victual, villain, violent, vow, vice, vulgar, vulture). "It would appear as if *v* is the most victorious letter, and when not victorious, the most vicious letter in the alphabet." Words dominated by *f* sounds are hardly less strong (fame, fear, fight, flame, furore, fury, festive, feast, food, filth, faith, famine, final, firm, fire, fury).

Just as gestures can be modified so as to introduce qualifying ideas of size, speed, distance, etc., so primitive tongues can be modified adjectivally. These alterations are metaphorically, if not actually, gestural in nature. Tylor has given us many instances. The Bachapin *héla* is a call or summons; the farther away the man who is hailed, the longer the *é* sound—*heela! he-e-la!* The Siamese word *non* ("there") can be made to indicate an object near or far according to the tonal accent. In Madagascar *ratchi* means "bad" and *râtchi* "very bad." The Watchandie say *boo-rie* for "small" *boo-rie-boo-rie* for "very small" and *b-o-rie-boorie* for "exceedingly small." Perhaps the best instances are found in Brazilian dialect, where *ouatou* means "stream" and *ijipakijiou* means "great." Hence the combination with lengthened vowels means river or *ouatou-ijiipakiiijou* while "*ouatou-iijipakiijou-ou-ou-ou-ou-ou*" stands for ocean. In the same way we can point to the almost universal employment of altered vowel-sounds to convey different ideas of distance (e.g. Javan: *iki* "this," *ika* "that" (intermediate) and *iker* "that" (far off); Japanese *-ko* "here" and *ka* "there"; French *ci* and *là*; German *dies* and *das*; English *this* and *that*). According to Westermann[1] the word *zo* (to walk) in the Ewe language can be accompanied by various adverbs which are almost gestural in nature. Thus they say *zo báfo báfo*, for the rapid steps of a man of short stature; *zo bèhe bèhe*, to drag one's feet along as from weakness; *zo bia bia*, the walk of a long-legged person; *zo boho boho*, the heavy tread of a fat man; *zo bula bula*, to stagger blindly; and *zo dzé dzé* to walk with swift energy. Abraham[2] also has mentioned that the spoken language of the Brazilian Puris is so meagre that gestures have to be added for the sake of comprehensibility. For the words "yesterday," "to-day," and "to-morrow" there is but one word "day." To indicate "yesterday" the Puris say "day" and point behind them; for "to-day" they say "day" and point to the sky and for "to-morrow" they say "day" and point forwards.

---

[1] Quoted by G. Dumas and A. Ombredane. "Les Mimiques: le langage," *Nouveau traité de psychol.* Tome iii. Fascic. 4. Paris. Alcan. 1937.
[2] Abraham, E. J. D., *The Story of the Deaf and the Dumb and the Language of Gesture.* Melbourne. (No date.)

CHAPTER III

THE NEUROLOGY OF GESTURE

CONSIDERATION of the clinical and anatomical aspects of gesture must be pursued along three distinct lines: (1) pantomime, (2) expressive movements, and (3) the cutaneous phenomena of blushing, goose-flesh, etc.

Pantomimic movements are deliberately executed actions of a high propositional content. Their integrity naturally demands an intactness of the final common pathway. Loss of pantomimic movements, however, may be seen in some lesions of the cerebral hemispheres, in the absence of any obvious paralysis. More rarely an exaggerated play of pantomime may occur. Whether any special regions of the brain are more significant than others in this respect is not yet fully known; whether both hemispheres share in this function or only the left is uncertain also. It seems, however, that some correlation exists between the zone of language in the left half of the brain and the execution of pantomimic movements.

In cases of aphasia due to focal cerebral lesions the part played by gesticulation forms an interesting if somewhat neglected subject. We may say at once that in the vast majority of cases, verbal speech suffers considerably more than gesture language. Even when the available vocabulary is grossly reduced, the aphasic patient can usually express himself clearly by means of pantomime. The meaning of such sign-movements is unmistakable even though the right upper extremity, by reason of paralysis, may not participate. Undoubtedly, however, in a large number of cases, the store of pantomime has suffered a depletion, and the mimicry falls short of normal standards in respect of richness and complexity. Thus a speechless aphasic patient cannot make his wants known as clearly as a patient who is rendered temporarily speechless from, sáy, an operation or painful affection of the mouth, tongue or jaw. In this way we observe that the damage to the speech-mechanism operates at an early point in the pre-verbal processes, and it is only in the slighter cases, where the immediately pre-verbal stages are defective, that one can regard the pantomime as approximately normal. Usually it can be stated that gesture suffers less than pantomime in cerebral speech affections.

For a moment one may stress those exceptional cases of aphasic speech-loss where the play of pantomimic movements is exaggerated. This may be observed in some cases of jargonaphasia where the patient is verbose but unintelligible; the speech strikes our ears as being a foreign language comprehended by the patient only, for the voice sinks and rises in a seemingly natural manner, the stress and emphasis falling in plausible cadences upon certain parts of the sentence. The jargon is usually accompanied by an excessive range of facial and manual gesticulation. Sometimes in cases of amnesic (or nominal) aphasia, the vocabulary is not obviously curtailed, and here, too, movements of gesture may be exaggerated. Goldstein[1] explains this fact by assuming that patients with amnesic aphasia have

[1] Goldstein, K. *Jour. Psychol.*, 1936, 2, 301.

lost their power of adopting a categorical (or abstract) attitude and that they talk and act solely along the lines of concrete behaviour. As he puts it, such patients "are not so much talking about the world as acting the part."

Again, in some long-standing cases of severe aphasia in young subjects, where the lesion is not a progressive one, a considerable amount of adjustment may take place within the patient's shrunken environment. The power of self-expression may develop along lines of gesture, with a considerable degree of attainment. Thus in a girl rendered almost entirely speechless by a cerebral embolism, the gesture-language was so evolved that she could inform her friends each day what doctors and visitors had seen her; she could answer the telephone, take messages and deliver them correctly to her sister; she often reminded her relatives of events which had taken place in her early childhood and which they had forgotten; all these complicated conversation pieces were effected mainly by way of an intricate dumb-show.

Exactly how the ability to propositionize by means of gesture is effected in the post-acute stages of an apoplectic aphasia, is not known. It is possible that other and unaffected regions of the left hemisphere may assume functions previously foreign to them and so enable the patient to express himself by means of signs. Equally if not more feasible is the view that the opposite hemisphere may take over expressive properties. Light would be thrown upon this problem by observing whether a second apoplectic insult located either within the left hemisphere or within the right has the effect of ablating the newly acquired functions of mimic self-expression.

In more complicated cases of aphasia, where both receptive and expressive aspects are involved, pantomime, and to a lesser extent gesture, obviously suffers. Lastly, in some profound cases of "total" aphasia with gross mental deterioration, there may be a complete defect of expression by means of signs. To connote this last type of case, Hamilton suggested to Hughlings Jackson the term "asemasia" from the Greek word "*semaino*"—"to express oneself by words or by signs." Jackson indeed at one time hazarded a clinical classification of the aphasias into: (1) disorder of speech, (2) loss of speech, and (3) loss of language, when pantomime and gesture as well as verbal speech are lacking.

There are special instances, which will be discussed later, where an elaboration of pantomime completely ousts verbalization from speech. The question then arises as to whether or not such a physiological shunting is associated with an anatomical substratum vulnerable to the usual morbid processes. In other words whether focal cerebral lesions, particularly of the left hemisphere, could damage or destroy the manual sign-language of, for example, the deaf-mute. That such might be the case was foreshadowed sixty years ago by Hughlings Jackson[1] who wrote: "No doubt, by disease of some part of the brain the deaf-mute might lose his natural system of signs which are of some speech-value to him."

Jackson's surmise has not, strictly speaking, yet been verified, but the record of a partial deaf-mute whose

[1] Jackson, Hughlings, *Brain*. 1878. I. 304.

ability to finger-spell became impaired after a stroke, suggests strongly that this form of communication may have a representation in the left cerebral hemisphere. This case was reported fully elsewhere (Critchley).[1] The literature contains no record of any other such case. Closest in approximation is the report made in 1896 by Grasset[2] of a deaf-mute who lost his ability to make hand-signs as the result of a cerebrovascular lesion. In Grasset's patient, however, the finger-spelling had ordinarily been carried out with the right hand only, as is the rule with deaf-mutes in France. Following the stroke, the patient could still execute finger-spelling correctly with the left hand, though scarcely at all with the right. Such an inconsistency suggests a different type of speech-affection than in my case, and is obviously to be regarded as an example of apraxia. An integrity of what may for the moment be termed rather loosely "internal speech" seems clear in Grasset's case and not in the other. Grasset came to the conclusion that in the cortex of the deaf-mute there exists a centre for manual speech which is independent of the motor area of the upper limb. He tentatively suggested the foot of the second frontal convolution as the possible site.

Gesture movements of the face and limbs belong to another physiological level and differ from pantomimic movements in their clinical and neuroanatomical correlates. Movements of gesture must be regarded as less voluntary and more automatic than those of pantomime. Their function qua speech

---

[1] Critchley, M., *Brain*. 1938. 61. 163.
[2] Grasset, *Le Prog. Méd.* 1896. 4. 281.

is one of emphasis rather than of replacement. Some representatives of this group indeed stand out as being still more automatic; such as the expressive movements of the face which accompany the act of speaking, or which may be in action independently of speech. Although not devoid of voluntary control, they are mainly outside the category of volitional activities.

The neurological status of these gesture movements need not be considered in any detail. Clinical experience shows that in certain morbid states they may be exaggerated or they may be lost. Exaggeration of expressive movements may be a feature of some diffuse or scattered disease-process within the cerebrum, such as vascular degeneration and disseminated sclerosis. It seems to be essential that both hemispheres of the brain should be affected. Some disorders of the basal ganglia, and more especially of the neostriatum, are characterized by exaggerated expressive movements. Examples are seen in Wilson's Disease and in chorea. Conversely, an impairment or loss of these movements may be observed in some other striatal diseases, especially when the pallidal system is affected, as in Parkinsonism. The occurrence of mimic paralysis of the face shows that hypomimia can be an affection which is not only unilateral but segmental. Better examples of generalized loss of movements of gesture and expression are adducible in certain psychoses, as, for example, catatonic schizophrenia.

The anatomical basis for such movements is uncertain. They certainly mediate by "private" projectional paths which are distinct from the pyramidal tract. Their site of origin is disputed, both the thalamus and the basal ganglia having been inculpated but without adequate evidence. It seems likely that the "private" path is a fronto-pontine fasciculus fringing in its course both globus pallidus and optic thalamus.

Next we have to consider the cutaneous phenomena, mainly affecting the face, which accompany expressive movements, although at times they may act as the sole objective evidence of emotion. In this way they can be regarded as vasomotor gestures. They differ from the pantomimic movements which have just been described (i) in that they are purely automatic and are to a large extent beyond the control of volition and (ii) that the neural mechanism lies in the autonomic nervous system. The phenomena are chiefly sympathetic, though to a minor degree parasympathetic, in nature. We must therefore look to the hypothalamus for the central representation of these functions.

Finally, reference should be made to those psychiatric cases where postures are inexplicably assumed and maintained. Examples are readily found in schizophrenics who adopt various bizarre and idiosignificant poses, or who make gestures of an esoteric nature. The same peculiarities are encountered in cases of primitive psychosis supervening upon a mental defect; they are conspicuous for instance in epiloiacs (Critchley and Earl).[1] It is probable that all these attitudes and mannerisms possess a meaning, which though obscure, may nevertheless yield to psychological methods of study.

[1] Critchley, M., and Earl, C. J. C., *Brain*. 1932. 55. 311.

CHAPTER IV

THE SIGN-TALK OF DEAF-MUTES

There are a number of very varied and interesting circumstances wherein spoken speech is either totally or partly in abeyance. An elaboration of pantomimic gestures may be evolved to serve as a means of communication, usurping the role of spoken speech. Thus arise various sign-languages, as they are called. The first of these circumstances is a pathological one where loss of hearing dating from birth or shortly afterwards precludes the development of speech. Despite this handicap deaf-mutes are by no means devoid of means of expressing themselves. In addition to their ability to follow the ideas of others by means of lip-reading, they possess a very important system of sign-talk of their own.

Incidentally, it is narrated by Sibscota, that when Cornelius Haga, ambassador of the United Provinces, reached Constantinople in the seventeenth century, he found that the mutes in the Sultan's seraglio had established a sign-language amongst themselves. Indeed it was on this account that the Osmanlis abandoned the practice of cutting out the tongues of their harem-attendants as being useless in ensuring discretion.

"Finger-spelling," "finger-talk," or "dactylology" is one of the chief means of symbolic formulation and expression at the disposal of the deaf-mute. We do not know with certainty where or how these systems arose. Certainly they were in use eight hundred years ago. It has been stated that there are references to finger-talk in the accounts of a deaf-mute cured in the seventh century by St. John of Beverley. The description of this healing as given by the Venerable Bede (*Eccles. Hist.*, vol. v, chap. ii) makes no mention, however, of gesture-language.

Credit is usually given to Charles Michel (the Abbé de l'Épée, 1712–89) who in 1759 opened in Paris a school for the education of the deaf and dumb. The finger-alphabet in its present form is usually ascribed to him and to his successor Roch Ambroise Cucurron (the Abbé Sicard). In France, however, a Spanish alphabet of the sixteenth century was embodied through the labours of Pereira and his deaf pupil Saboureaux de Fontenay, from the original work of the Benedictine monk, Pedro Ponce de Leon (1520–84). Rather earlier the way was prepared by the teachings of Jerome Cardano (1501–75), who rebelled against the current acceptance of Aristotle's teaching, that connected thought was impossible without speech.

Here and there we catch glimpses of various older systems of finger-speech, some of which perished unnoticed, while others are to-day found incorporated in accepted usage. In 1692 La Fin,[1] one-time secretary to Cardinal Richelieu, advocated a "silent language," executed by pointing towards various parts of the body. Thus the five vowels were to be indicated by touching the thumb to each finger-tip in turn, while the hollow of the hand stood for *y*.

[1] La Fin, *Sermo mirabilis, or the Silent Language*. London. 1692.

The remainder of the alphabet was signed as follows: *b*, brow; *c*, cheek; *d*, the deaf ear; *f*, forehead; *g*, gullet; *h*, hair; *k*, knuckle; *l*, legs; *m*, mouth; *n*, nose; *p*, pap; *r*, rib; *s*, shoulder; *t*, temples; *v*, vein in arm; *w*, wrist; *x*, two index fingers crossed; *z*, lower part of the breast; *q* was to be represented by any quick movement. One of the obvious shortcomings of this alphabet was its applicability to the English language only, and La Fin therefore constructed a second language for use in Latin. La Fin's proposition was never accepted, and a few years later a pamphlet entitled *Digiti Lingua* advocated a return to a manual alphabet such as we recognize to-day.[1]

Bishop Wilkins[2] of Chester suggested in 1694 another form of manual speech. The tops of the fingers should signify the five vowels; the middle parts, the first five consonants; the bottom parts, the next five. The spaces between the fingers were to represent the next four consonants. One finger laid on the side of the hand might stand for *t*, two fingers *v*, three *w*, the little finger crossed *x*, the wrist *y*, and the middle part of the hand *z*.

We also find a reference to the gesture-language of deaf-mutes in 1644 when Bulwer[3] wrote: ". . . that wonder of necessity which Nature worketh in men that are borne deafe and dumbe; who can argue and dispute rhetorically by signes, and with a kind

---

[1] *Digiti Lingua*. Anon. London. 1698.
[2] Wilkins, J., "Mercury, or the Secret and Swift Messenger," from the collected *Mathematical and Philosophical Works*, vol. II. London. 1802.
[3] Bulwer, J., *Chirologia, or the Naturall Language of the Hand*. London. 1644.

of mute and logistique eloquence overcome their amaz'd oponents; wherein some are so ready excellent, they seeme to want nothing to have their meanings perfectly understood." We read too, in Montaigne,[1] a brief mention of "alphabets upon fingers, and Grammars by gestures."

To-day both in France and in the U.S.A. the original alphabet of the Abbé de l'Épée is taught. It differs from that used in England and elsewhere in being unimanual. Thus in France, Italy and the U.S.A. the right hand alone is employed in making signs. This is because early in the nineteenth century the Abbé Sicard collaborated with the Rev. T. H. Gallaudet of Connecticut, in introducing into America methods of educating deaf-mutes. The deaf instructor, Laurent Clerc, left Paris to take charge of the first Gallaudet school for the deaf, founded in 1817 in Hartford, Conn. In the United Kingdom the training of the deaf and dumb developed along independent lines, and for some time during the middle of the eighteenth century it was monopolized by the Braidwood family of Edinburgh who refused to associate with the Paris school of instruction. The familiar mode of communication with deaf-mutes is of course by means of this dactylology or finger-spelling, either on one hand or on both. Either method is rapid of execution. An adept operator of the two-hand alphabet can spell fifty words to the minute. The unimanual system is even faster, and Helen Keller, for example, could spell and sign eighty words a minute.

[1] Montaigne, *Essays*, vol. II. chap. xii.

Besides these methods of dactylology, all deaf-mutes possess another and lesser known system, which is a kind of manual shorthand, whereby a single gesture stands not for a letter but for a word, a phrase, or even a sentence. This variety of sign-language, although practised by all deaf-mutes, is largely unfamiliar to outsiders and indeed many are unaware of its very existence. The language is not committed to text-books, nor is it taught in schools; and except for a few obscure pamphlets [1-7], there is practically no literature upon the subject. It is handed on from one deaf-mute to another as a sort of tradition or it may be picked up in their institutions. Very probably it was bound up with the system of the Abbé de l'Épée, who incorporated in part this natural system already in universal use. The less instructed the deaf-mute, the greater the proportion of "natural" signs, though the total vocabulary will be small. Most training-schools have their own private code of arbitrary symbols, which are included within the general stock. It therefore comes about that the educated deaf-mute employs natural signs, conventional symbols and finger-spelling, so that he possesses eventually a rich and elastic vocabulary capable of expressing abstractions,

[1] Green, B. P., *A Handbook in the Manual Alphabet, and the Sign-language of the American Deaf*. Ohio. 1916.
[2] Higgins, D. D., *How to talk to the Deaf*. No date.
[3] Michaels, J. W., *A handbook of the Sign-language of the Deaf*. Atalanta. 1923.
[4] Abraham, E. J. D., *loc. cit.*
[5] Long, J. Schuyler. *The Sign Language*. Des Moines. 1918.
[6] Neale, A. J. and Fry, M. S., *The Language of the Silent World*. Cardiff. No date.
[7] Payne, A. H., quoted in the *Lancet*. 1937. i. 700.

shades of meaning, and even witticisms. It has been noted that very young deaf-mutes are able to communicate freely with each other through the medium of a very rich store of gestures and facial mimicry. That these movements are "instinctive" in nature is suggested by their presence at an age prior to the beginnings of systematic instruction.

Two interesting features attach themselves to this sign-language. In the first place it is economical and rapid, so that it can be executed or read three times as quickly as articulate speech. It is potentially graceful and pleasing to the eye, and a wide range of expressive or facial movements can accompany and enrich the manual signs in a manner which is supremely eloquent. Payne[1] has even gone so far as to acclaim it far more expressive, facile and beautiful than the English of Shakespeare or the Bible.

Of greater interest is the fact that this manual speech is largely "international" and surmounts the barriers erected by race, religion or language. In other words there is a striking similarity—often an identity—between the gestures employed by deaf-mutes of different nationality. That is not to say that differences do not occur, as indeed may be found between deaf-mutes taught in different institutions in the same city. This is largely due to the local arbitrary symbols which are taught. Nevertheless the differences are not fundamental, and deaf-mutes of all countries readily understand each other. In a school for the deaf and dumb in Budapest, a

[1] Payne, A. H., *loc. cit.*

number of children from France, Austria, Czechoslovakia and Italy were admitted as temporary delegates. Within an hour or two they were all communicating freely with each other and at the end of a day it was as though they had been brought up together. In 1935 a service was held in St. Paul's Cathedral attended by deaf-mutes from fourteen different countries; the sermon which was delivered entirely in sign-language was readily understood by all.[1]

Abraham,[2] the Australian instructor of deaf-mutes, tells us that he found no difficulty in communicating by way of signs with deaf subjects from France, Italy, Germany, Norway and Sweden. In London he spent a day with three Italian deaf-mute visitors; he showed them the sights, travelled with them and never was there any trouble in understanding or being understood.

Some of the signs may be regarded as "instinctive gestures" in that they are obvious, and possess a symbolism which is universally accepted and employed. Thus, touching or patting the stomach denotes "hunger"; an index finger applied to the brow means "to think"; when this finger taps the forehead or makes small circular motions the meaning changes to "crazy." Two fingers of the right hand applied to the radial pulse at the left wrist indicates "doctor." These symbols all belong to the category of "natural signs" either because they mimic the natural appearance or action of the object concerned,

[1] Paget, Sir R. *Nature*. 1936. *137*. 384.
[2] Abraham, E. J. D., *loc. cit.*

or else because they are so habitual as to be self-evident.

Some other of the signs are more obscure and are apparently empirical in origin. Thus it is not easy to understand why pinching the lobe of the left ear should denote "yellow." Nevertheless there may well be a rational explanation for the form-pattern of every one of the gestures in this universal sign-language, however cryptic. Thus the sign for "cake" is made by inverting the right hand and placing the finger-tips upon the back of the left hand, the palm being downward; the explanation of this gesture possibly lies in the fact that this attitude represents someone holding the cake steadily in order to cut it. Again the sign for "new" is made by holding the left palm inward, fingers pointing to the right, and the right palm inward with fingers to the left. The right hand is then slid along the back of the left. This gesture possibly represents new metal being pushed out of a mould.

The sign-language of deaf-mutes possesses its own primitive syntax. Definite and indefinite articles are usually omitted; adjectives and verbs are not easily distinguished. The tenses are not differentiated unless the meaning of the phrase absolutely demands this. The order of words is logical rather than in conformity with local grammatical construction. Thus instead of the sentence "a dark, handsome man rides and walks," one would sign: "Man—dark—handsome—ride—walk"; for "bring a black hat"—"hat black bring." "I am hungry, give me bread."—"hungry, bread me give." The

Lord's Prayer would be signed as follows: "Father our, heaven in—name thy hallowed—kingdom thy come—will thy done—earth on, heaven in, as. Bread give us daily—trespasses our forgive us, them trespass against us, forgive, as. Temptation lead not—but evil deliver from—kingdom power glory thine for ever."

A good deal of facial expressive movements usually embellishes the sign-talk. Indeed deaf-mutes are at times seen to communicate with each other while one arm is engaged in holding a parcel; or even while both hands are in their pockets.

There is a tale concerning the high efficiency of facial mimicry practised and understood by deaf-mutes. Gallaudet assured the painter Trumbull that he could portray any well-known event in history, simply by facial gesture, in such a way that his deaf and dumb pupils would comprehend. Trumbull selected the Roman story of Brutus condemning his two sons to death for insubordination. Folding his arms, Gallaudet enacted this event simply by expressive movements of the face and trunk, and each deaf and dumb member of the audience understood and named the event correctly.

It is also interesting to note that when two or more deaf-mutes are in animated conversation they evince in addition to their rapid sign-talk, odd little grunting, whining, whimpering, and twittering noises, which are of course inaudible to themselves. When pleased, the deaf-mute may emit a sort of cat-like purring; Laura Bridgman would hiss when annoyed. These primitive utterances occurring among a speechless gesture-making community may be of the greatest significance in our conceptions of the origins of verbal speech in man. We see here not only the traces of an interjectional beginning of language (pooh-pooh hypothesis) but even something still more primitive, namely, the operation of crude muscular movements rendered audible (yo-heave-ho theory.)

CHAPTER V

SIGN-LANGUAGE AMONG THE NORTH-AMERICAN INDIANS

STUDENTS of gesture immediately turn to those systems of sign-talk practised by the aboriginal habitants of the North American continent from the Gulf of Mexico to the Hudson. Within this vast area there can be distinguished about sixty-five linguistic families, differing radically in speech one from the other. Within each family there may exist a number—sometimes as many as twenty—separate tongues. These linguistic obstacles were overcome by the employment of a *lingua franca* of signs used when tribesmen met for the chase, barter, counsel or attack. Such sign-talk had the additional merit of speed, for a skilled exponent can converse about three times as quickly with signs as with speech.

Where this sign-talk originated is uncertain, but tradition points to the South. The interpreter Clark has said that the Cheyennes ascribe the sign-language to the Kiowas, who brought it from Mexico. The date of origin is also not known. Certainly gesture was freely employed at the time of the coming of the first explorers in the fifteenth century as testified by the original accounts of the voyages of discovery. All records made by the earliest traders and settlers confirm this view.

The sign-language of the North American Indians has been studied by comparatively few. First among the publications dealing with this subject is S. H. Long's work, which appeared in 1823 and gave descriptions of about one hundred signs. Garrick Mallery[1] in 1880 and 1881 published two works on this problem from the Bureau of American Ethnology (Smithsonian Institute). These two monographs incidentally constitute the most scholarly treatise upon the whole subject of gesture that has been published. There followed W. Philo Clark's posthumous work[2] published in 1885, and later, three books appearing in 1887, 1890 and 1893, written by Lewis F. Hadley. Ernest Thompson Seton's well-illustrated work[3] appeared in 1918 and has been followed by the illuminating *Universal Indian Sign Language* of Wm. Tomkins (1926).[4]

This sign-language is readily comprehended by Indians living in areas far removed from each other. Minor differences occur, but they are insufficient to hinder mutual comprehension. Little Raven, who was chief of the Southern Arapahoes, has said: "The summer after President Lincoln was killed, we had a grand gathering of all the tribes to the East and South of us. Twenty-five different tribes met near old Fort Abercombie on the Wichita River. The Caddos had a different sign for horse, and also for moving, but the rest were made the same by all the tribes." Two well-marked dialectic groups are said to exist: the Northern, where the whole hand and

---

[1] Mallery, Garrick, Bureau American Ethnol., Smithsonian Instit. 1880–1881.
[2] Clark, W. Philo, *The Indian Sign Language*. Philadelphia. 1885.
[3] Seton, E. Thompson, *Sign Talk*. New York. 1918.
[4] Tomkins, W., *Universal Indian Sign Language*. San Diego. 1926.

both hands are freely employed; and the Southern, which is largely a uni-manual and finger system. The former of these is better suited for purposes of signalling; the latter for conversation. The Cheyenne Indians are usually looked upon as the best exponents of sign-talk, followed closely by their neighbours, the Arapahoes. Others give the credit to the Kiowas.

The Indian sign-talk has of course, its own primitive syntax and its own logical word-sequence. This is well illustrated in the following example taken from Tomkins:

> *English* "Two months ago I took two friends with me and went up to start the camp. The day we got there we saw tracks of deer and bear, and caught some fish for supper. We were too tired when night came to put up our tents, and we didn't think it would rain anyway. We made up our beds near the fire and lay down to sleep."
>
> *Indian* "Two moon beyond I with two friend go make-rise camp. We arrive little-hand; we see track deer, bear; we take fish eat sunset. Evening come we tired, we want not make-rise tent; we think rain no. We make bed near fire, sleep."

The North American Indians are also adept in the art of making static gestures out of inanimate objects, that is, sign-making. A twig bent or placed in a certain position may serve as a symbol or indication. Amongst such signs, Garrick Mallery has given us:

> *A stick pointing in a particular direction* = "I have gone this way."
> *Another stick crossing the above at a right angle* = the distance travelled, whether long or short.

NORTH-AMERICAN INDIANS 45

Cutting the bark off a tree on = "I have had bad (very bad,
one, two, three or four sides   dreadful) luck."
Cutting off the bark all round = "I am starving."
Smoking a piece of birch-bark
and hanging it on a tree = "I am ill."

It is an interesting and not altogether unexpected observation that there is a most striking similarity between the sign-languages of the North American Indians and of the deaf and dumb. This is a fact which has been repeatedly confirmed and which can be readily verified by comparing the illustrations in Mallery's report with one of the rare manuals for the instruction of deaf-mutes. Indians can communicate without any difficulty with the deaf; according to Mallery there may be initial disagreements between the signs, but they are mutually comprehensible, and signs of one system are often adopted by adherents of the other. In 1880, the same writer took a number of Ute Indians to the National Deaf-mute College at Washington, where a very high degree of reciprocal intelligibility was found.

One difference between the two systems is that the deaf-mute enhances his gestures with lively facial movements, whereas the Indian's countenance remains grave and impassive. Perhaps too, the Indian's sign-talk is less concerned with words than with ideas. Possibly also, the Indian's use of metaphor renders his sign-talk of higher æsthetic worth than the others.

CHAPTER VI

SIGN-TALK AMONG AUSTRALIAN ABORIGINES

YET another system of sign-talk is known amongst a primitive society, namely in Australian bush-dwellers especially in North-West Queensland. Although this language has not received the same attention as in the case of the American Indians, Roth[1] has published a most comprehensive anthropological monograph upon the Pitta-Pitta tribes of that region. Therein he discussed in some detail their language and dialects.

According to Roth, the Pitta-Pitta aborigines, who inhabit the Boulia district of the interior of Queensland, employ a sign-language in addition to their own articulate speech. Roth prefers to regard this system as a collection of "ideagrams," each sign conjuring up an idea which may be modified according to the context. Thus the sign for a boomerang may not only serve to represent the object itself, but also the circumstances of its employment, e.g. hitting or killing something by its means, or making, bartering, stealing a boomerang. The aboriginal uses the sign-language when travelling amongst strangers, and also when on the warpath or the chase, where silence becomes a necessity. There is evidence too, that these ideagrams are employed on certain ceremonial occasions, as for instance,

[1] Roth, W. E., *Ethnological Studies among the North-West-Central Queensland Aborigines.* Brisbane. 1897.

during the first initiation rites of the adolescent males. Most of the Pitta-Pitta signs are made with the hands, but some of them are executed with the head and face only. In this way nodding movements serve to express negation or affirmation; sniffing indicates the odour of the wild-orange; biting of the beard expresses anger; and pouting of the lips in a particular quarter indicates direction. One or two of the signs are executed with the trunk; shrugging of the shoulders stands for doubt or interrogation, while the supreme insult which one Pitta-Pitta woman can offer another is expressed by a forward-protrusion of the abdomen with exposure of the person, followed by a vibration of the knees and thighs one against the other, the heels being kept together.

Roth describes in his monograph a series of two hundred and thirteen ideagrams, ranging from the depiction of plants and animals, to concepts of an abstract character.

One year previously Stirling[1] had investigated and described the gesture-language used in Central Australia by the Arunta and Luritcha tribes. He was of opinion that sign-talk was even more widely diffused throughout that Continent. In attempting to learn and copy these gestures, Stirling and his colleagues found a little difficulty in the actual manipulation of the fingers, and the white men could in no way attain the nimbleness of execution shown by the natives. Stirling's monograph contains

[1] Stirling, E. C., *Report on the Work of the Horn Scientific Expedition to Central Australia*. Part IV. London and Melbourne. 1896.

a list of hand-signs, many of which are illustrated. His chief instructor was a Luritcha aboriginal from Temple Downs, but he was able to incorporate a number of gestures which his colleague Mr. Gillen learned from an Arunta native belonging to Alice Springs, and some which Professor Spencer had picked up from a native at Ayers Rock. Certain differences are seen, but members of adjoining tribes seem, in practice, to be able to understand each other's signs.

Howitt[1,2] has also studied the gesture-language of Australian aborigines. He found considerable variation in the use of signs even within a small area. Thus, some communities have very extensive gesture-vocabularies, while neighbouring tribes may employ few signs if any. Again, the circumstances under which gestures are made differ very much. Among the Dieri, for instance, a widow is not permitted to speak until the mourning layer of white clay with which she has plastered herself has peeled off. During this period—which may be one of months—she communicates by gesture only.

It is of interest to compare the codes employed by a number of the Australian natives:

All Right.

Pitta-Pitta	The fingers are loosely hooked at the proximal joints: a single vertical flexion from the elbow.
Aldolinga	Hold the hand out, palm upwards, and describe several circles with it.
Kuriwalu	Nod the head twice.

[1] Howitt, A. W., *Proc. Austr. Assoc. Adv. Sci.* for 1890 (1891). 2. 637–646.
[2] Idem, *Native Tribes of South-East Australia.* London and New York. 1904.

Drink Water.

Wurunjerri	Imitate lifting water to the mouth with the hand.
Dieri	Place the thumb and forefinger of the right hand together like a scoop and carry the hand up to the mouth.
Kuriwalu	Throw the head back, and carry the hand up to the mouth.
Geo. Gill Range	Fist loosely closed, thumb uppermost and only slightly bent. Hand in this position jerked two or three times towards the ulnar side.
Pitta-Pitta	Lapping up of water, in handfuls.

Horse.

Geo. Gill Range	Lightly clenched fist, palm down, is moved up and down with slight movements; flexion and extension from the wrist.
Pitta-Pitta	Fingers closely apposed and all flexed at proximal joints with tips just touching palm; wrist flexed. Forwards and backwards movement from elbow to show the flat hoofs coming to the ground in rhythmic succession.
Mitakoodi	Finger tips touching the top of the thumb; inward rotatory movements at the wrist.

Paget[1] has compared some of the signs employed by the Pitta-Pitta people with the symbol representing the same idea, as used by the Red Indians and the deaf and dumb. He found a striking similarity between some of the signs contained in these three systems.

Paget also refers to a sign language existing in Russian Armenia and the Caucasus, and practised

---

[1] Paget, Sir R., *Sign Language as a Form of Speech*. Paper read at the Royal Institute of Great Britain. Dec. 13th, 1935.

by the men-folk alone. Here too, a similarity was found with the gestures of the deaf-mute, the Red Indians and the Australian aborigines. Three examples were given by Paget, viz:

Man: a beard-sign (as in the Australian and deaf-mute systems).
Woman: a head-dress sign (also in deaf-mute gestures).
Water: a cupped hand raised to the mouth (as in Red-Indian sign-talk).

The same author also mentioned the discovery of a sign-language in the Cameroons. This is practised especially in the native courts of justice where disputants of many tribes and tongues are interrogated.

CHAPTER VII
SIGN-LANGUAGE IN RELIGIOUS COMMUNITIES

OCCASIONALLY for reasons of religious discipline, articulate speech is forsworn or forbidden, and in such circumstances, elaborate gestures constitute the only means of inter-communication. In a number of Roman monastic orders a rule of silence is imposed. This observance is most strictly and consistently applied in the case of the Order of Cistercians of the Strict Observance, better known as the "Trappists." Among this community, writing is forbidden, and speech is permitted only at certain hours between a monk and his abbot. A complex sign-language has developed, however, which goes far to circumvent the spirit if not the letter of their rule. Silence also formed one of the austerities practised by other cenobites, as for example, the original Cistercians of Cîteaux. It was probably enjoined on occasions at least, among the early Benedictines and also in their Cluniac offshoot, and possibly in other orders as well.[1, 2]

Although there are not many published accounts of the sign-language in monastic communities, the Florentine monk Rossellius in 1576 described three such alphabets. Leibnitz[3] (1768) gave a description

[1] Grolleau, C. and Chastel, G., *L'Ordre de Citeaux; la Trappe.* 1932. Paris.
[2] Anon., *La Trappe in England.* 1937. London.
[3] Leibnitz, G. G., *Opera Omnia.* Vol. vi. Part 2. Geneva. 1768. p. 207.

of a large number of signs employed by Cistercian monks for the purposes of communication. In 1726 the Abbé Herrgot,[1] in his *Vetus Disciplina Monastica*, recorded fully a series of 460 signs used by certain Benedictine monks. In 1840 Aungier[2] tabulated a number of the signs utilized by the Sisters and Brethren of the Bridgettine double monastery of Syon.

The Trappist code of manual signs has apparently been handed down from the customs of Cluny (A.D. 910). In 1824, Dubois[3] published anonymously a history of the Abbey of La Trappe, and therein he described a sign-vocabulary of some 167 words in common use. A comparison of some of the gestures described by Dubois and by Herrgot may be of interest:

[1] Herrgot, *Vetus disciplina monastica*. Paris. 1726.
[2] Aungier, G. J., *A History of Antiquities of Syon Monastery in the Parish of Isleworth*. London. Nichols. 1840. p. 405.
[3] Dubois, L., *Histoire civile, religieuse et litteraire de l'abbaye de la Trappe*. Paris. 1824.

	Trappist (Dubois)	Benedictine (Herrgot)
Water	Clasp the five fingers.	Join together all the fingers of the right hand, and move them sideways.
Holy water	Clasp the five fingers of the left hand and make a cross above with the thumb of the right hand.	To the general sign, add the sign of the cross with the hand opened out.
Mass	Make the signs for *bread* and for *wine* and then the sign of the cross.	Sign of the cross with the hand extended.
Master of the Novices	Touch the first finger with the little one.	Draw the hand across the hair by the forehead (which is the sign for *novice* and for anything *new*) and add the sign for *seeing*.
Prior	Show the extended thumb.	Imitate holding and ringing a bell with two fingers.
Bread	Extend two fingers and the thumb so as to form a triangle.	Make a circle with both thumbs and the first two fingers.
Eggs	Scratching a finger.	With the finger of one hand, imitate a person picking the shell off an egg.
Wine	Touch the nose with the end of the first finger.	Bend the finger and put it to the lips.
Speaking	Curve the finger and put it to the mouth.	Hold the hand in front of the mouth and move it in an opening and shutting manner.
Negation	Show all the fingers except the thumb.	Place the tip of the middle finger under the thumb, and make it spring forwards.
Dead	Put the index finger under the chin.	Draw finger across the thumb.

CHAPTER VIII
SIGN-LANGUAGE: SECRET SOCIETIES

The employment of signs and gestures often reaches great elaboration when incorporated within the workings of occult communities. Secret societies, with their various aims, codes, hierarchies, initiation rites, symbols, passwords and cryptic signs, have existed since the beginnings of human records.[1] By reason of their essential nature of secrecy, little is known of most of these sign-languages. It is incontestable that secret signs played important roles in some occult religions, as that of Mithra (J. F. Maternus[2]); of sects such as the Gnostics and the Ophites (C. W. King[3], R. Payne Knight[4]), and the modern Ansars and Ansayrii of Asia Minor (Walpole[5]). It is believed by Lloyd[6] and others that the Mudrās or symbolic hand-gestures forming part of Hindū and Buddhist ritual, were derived from the Gnostic sects of Egypt. They also participated in certain semi-religious bodies such as the Knights Templar and the original Rosicrucians.

In the Middle Ages there were a number of professional guilds, of a secret nature, wherein

[1] Lepper, J. W., *Famous Secret Societies*. London. (No date.)
[2] Maternus, J. F., *De erroribus profanarum religionum*.
[3] King, C. W., *The Gnostics and their Remains*. London. 1864.
[4] Knight, R. P., *Symbolic Language of Ancient Art and Mythology*. New York. 1876.
[5] Walpole, Hon. F. T., *The Ansayrii and the Assassins*. Vol. 3, p. 354. London. 1851.
[6] Lloyd, A., *The Creed of Half Japan*.

sign-symbolism was included. Such were the Steinmetzen and the Fenderers (or Hewers). Criminal classes too, have had their secret societies, each with its appropriate ritual, as exemplified by the medieval Gueux and Mercelots in France; the Upright Men of Tudor England; the Black Hand in the U.S.A.; the Camorra of Naples; the Mafia of Sicily (at present under a Fascist cloud); and the Thugs or Phansegars of India. We might even include here the brotherhood of the Ku Klux Klan. Most secret societies have had political or anarchistic motives, which have brought them in conflict with established authority. Of the large number of such societies may be mentioned the Illuminati; les Philadelphes; the Carbonari (both of Naples and of France); Les Droits de l'Homme; the Hetairia of Greece; the Spanish Communeros; the United Slavonians of Russia; and the Polish Templars. Many of these societies were intermingled or associated with continental Lodges of Freemasonry. Ireland was the home of a large number of secret societies, mainly subversive in political aim, but also outlets for lawlessness. The names of the Whiteboys; the Oakboys; the Hearts of Steel; the Protestant Ribbonmen, the Orange Society and the Peep-of-Day Boys; the United Irishmen; and the Fenians suggest themselves.

Oddly enough, it is concerning the Chinese secret societies that most information is available. In addition to Three Kingdoms, the Red Beards, the White Jackets, the Short Swords, the Society of Glory and Splendour, the Sea and Land Society, and the White Water Lilies, the most widely known society is that of the Boxers. This word is a misreading of The Fist for the Protection of Public Peace (see Wilhelm[1]; T'ang Leang-Li[2]; Sun-Yat-Sen[3]).

Of greatest interest from the aspect of sign-language is that Chinese secret brotherhood known as the Hung or Triad Society, (also known as the Society of Heaven and Earth, or the Society of Brothers and Elders.[4—6]) Although its origins cannot be traced further back than 1662, its symbolization can be directly connected with ancient mysteries, and the signs can be readily linked up with the original *mantras* or spells which served to convey ideas not easily put into words. Members of the Hung Society make use of a complex system of hand-signs by which they can converse with each other in secrecy, not unlike the deaf and dumb. In addition, various bodily postures and manual attitudes are brought into their ceremonies, and furthermore serve to establish membership and to convey signals or messages when amongst outsiders.

Thus, the general pass-sign consists in a stretching out of the right hand with all the fingers extended and abducted. The esoteric meaning of this gesture is a reference to the five ancestors and also to the five senses of man. Another gesture is one of

[1] Wilhelm, R., *The Soul of China*.
[2] T'ang Leang-Li, *Inner History of the Chinese Revolution*. London. 1930.
[3] Sun-Yat-Sen, *Memoirs of a Chinese Revolutionary*. London. 1927.
[4] Kesson, J., *The Cross and the Dragon*. London. 1854.
[5] Ward, J. S. M. and Stirling, W. G., *The Hung Society*. 3 vols. London. 1925.
[6] Tomlin, *Jour. Roy. Asiatic Soc.* Vol. iv. p. 137.

touching the tip of the second finger with the thumb, which symbolizes the pricking of the finger carried out during the ceremony of initiation. There are also signs to represent the five elements:

Gold: the arms are raised above the head with the palms touching, and then lowered to the sides.
Wood: forearms are crossed in front of the abdomen.
Earth: the hands point inwards towards the pit of the stomach, the back of the finger-tips being in contact. The knees may be semiflexed.
Fire: the arms are first raised above the head with the elbow joints slightly bent; they are then brought to the sides in three stages.
Water: the backs of the hands rest upon the hips, the elbows bent somewhat.

The "Sign of Heaven and Earth" is made with the index finger of the right hand directed upwards and that of the left hand pointing downwards. There is also a three-phase sign meaning: "I am a Heaven and Earth man."

When a street fight is in progress—an important eventuality in the case of a semi-political fraternity—members of the Hung Society can give signs to indicate that a participant is or is not a brother.

Members also extend their system of signs to include the employment of inanimate objects. This mode of signalling reaches heights of great elaborateness. They have their own methods of holding their hats; of placing their shoes on the doorstep; of carrying a stick or umbrella; of lighting a cigarette; or offering or accepting a cigarette or a box of matches. There exists a complicated language of the tea-table, whereby a varying arrangement of cups and teapots can carry on a prolonged conversation, without a word being uttered. Other groupings of domestic articles can become eloquent. When rioting is afoot, a member places on his doorstep a large bowl of water, across which is laid a knife and on this a small cup of water. When a member enters a house he holds his pig-tail in the right hand and slowly twists it from left to right. Should his object be to borrow money, he accepts a cup of tea offered him, but instead of drinking it, he places it at the corner of the table. If the householder is willing to lend, he silently raises the cup and drains it; otherwise he quietly moves the cup untasted to the centre of the table.

CHAPTER IX

SIGN-LANGUAGE IN ORIENTAL LITERATURE

ORIENTAL literature illustrates the importance of symbolic gesture, not only as a part of ritual in religion, but also in folk-lore and even in workaday uses of daily life. The extreme elaboration of gesture seen in the dance and stagecraft of the Indian and Chinese theatre will be considered in greater detail later.

In ancient India a language of signs was in common currency as it is to-day, though the services of an adept were often required for the interpretation of the more obscure symbols. Inanimate objects were often employed to enrich still more the vocabulary. Tawney tells us that at the outbreak of the Indian Mutiny the signal for revolt was spread by the distribution of such articles as griddle-cakes or lotus-blossom. On occasion spears, arrows, sticks, twigs may also serve as signalling devices. (Such practices recall the Chinese use of chop-sticks in conveying messages and also the Peruvian knotted strings or *quipus*. Throughout Europe, the gypsies make use of an arrangement of sticks placed in the roadway, as indicators of various types.) In India, according to Crooke, the gift of a leaf of pān with betel and sweet spices inside means "I love you." If large amounts of spice are contained, and one corner is turned down in a peculiar way, it signifies "come." When tumeric is added, the meaning is,

"I cannot come," and if a piece of charcoal is included the message reads: "Go, I have done with you."

Incidents from the Hindu *Ocean of Story*[1] illustrate the Indian sign-language. In chapter v., vol. i, we read: "Once upon a time Yogananda went outside the city, and beheld in the middle of the Ganges, a hand, the five fingers of which were closely pressed together. That moment he summoned one and said, 'What does this mean?' But I displayed two of my fingers in the direction of the hand. Thereupon the hand disappeared, and the King, exceeding astonished, again asked me what this meant, and I answered him: 'That hand meant to say, by showing its five fingers: "what cannot five men united effect in this world?" Then I, King, showed it these two fingers, wishing to indicate that nothing is impossible when even two men are of one mind.'"

Again in the seventh chapter we find the story of Pushpadanta . . . "she came out of the women's apartments, and took with her teeth a flower and threw it down to him. He, not understanding this mysterious sign made by the princess, puzzled as to what he ought to do, went home to his preceptor. . . . Then the clever preceptor guessed the riddle, and said to him: 'By letting drop a flower with her tooth she made a sign to you that you were to go to this temple rich in flowers, called Pushpadanta, and wait there.'"

The sixth volume also contains the story of the

[1] Penzer, N. M., *The Ocean of Story*. 10 vols. London. 1926.

Pānwpattī Rānī, which is full of symbolism. We read that the Rānī puts a rose between her teeth, then behind her ear and then lays it at her feet. These actions signify, first, that her name was Rājā Dant or Rājā Tooth. The rose laid behind her ear signifies that she came from the land of Karnātak, which literally means "on the ear"; the rose at her feet represented her name, Pānwpatti or "Foot-leaf."

Penzer also refers to a story in the Mongolian Arji-Borji Khan, wherein Naran, a rigidly chaperoned princess, signals from her balcony to the minister Ssaran. She holds up one finger and encircles it with her other hand; then she clasps her hands together and separates them. After that she places two fingers together and with them points towards the palace. The interpretation of this symbolism was given as follows: the upraised finger means to convey the idea of a tree and the encircling action, a wall. Clasping and unclasping the hands was an invitation to enter the flower garden and the juxtaposition of two fingers was a sign that she would welcome a visit.

Other allusions in Oriental literature can be found outside India, and especially in Moslem countries. A few more direct quotations from Eastern literature may be used in illustration. Thus, in the Tale of the Goldsmith—from Hatim's[1] songs and stories —we read: "... he made two balls of gold and went out holding (these and other) balls in his hand. Hither and thither he pitched balls of stone and balls of iron as he went along, till he came below the

[1] *Hatim's Tales.* A. Stein and G. A. Grierson. London. 1923.

princess's window, and through it he flung into her lap-cloth the two balls of gold. On this she turned her back towards him and showed him a mirror. Then she threw some water out of the window. Then she threw out a posy of flowers, and again a hair. Finally she lifted up an iron stiletto and with it scratched the sill of the window." The goldsmith's wife interpreted the princess's actions thus: "When she turned her back and showed the mirror, she meant that someone else was there: when she threw out water she meant that you must come in by the water drain; when she threw the posy of flowers she meant that it was the garden into which you must come; when she showed the stiletto she meant that you must bring a file, as there are iron railings to be cut through; and when she threw a hair, she meant that she was combing her locks."

Illustrations may also be taken from the *Arabian Nights Entertainments*.[1] The Tale of Aziz and Azizah narrates: "When unexpectedly there fell on me from above a white kerchief, softer to the touch than the morning breeze and pleasanter to the sight than healing to the diseased. I hent it in hand and raised my head to see whence it had fallen, when my eyes met the eyes of the lady who owned these gazelles ... and lo! she was looking out of a wicket in a lattice of brass and never saw my eyes a fairer than she; and in fine, tongue faileth to describe her beauty. When she caught sight of me looking at her, she put her forefinger into her mouth, then

---

[1] *Arabian Nights Entertainments*, vol. ii. Burton Edition. 17 vols. (No date.)

joined her middle finger and witness-finger (Arab. *shahid* the *index*, the pointer raised in testimony; the comparison of the Eastern and Western names is curious), and laid them on her bosom, between her breasts; after which she drew in her head and closed the wicket-shutter and went her ways. . . . I abode perplexed for that I heard no word by her spoken, nor understood the meaning of her token. . . . Then she asked me, 'What said she, and what signs made she to thee?' I answered, 'She uttered not a word, but put her forefinger to her mouth, then joining it to her middle finger, laid both fingers on her bosom and pointed to the ground. Thereupon she withdrew her head and shut the wicket; and after that I saw her no more. However, she took my heart with her, so I sat till sundown, expecting her again to look out of the window; but she did it not; and, when I despaired of her, I rose from my seat and came home. This is my history and I beg thee to help me in this my sore calamity.' Upon this she raised her face to me and said: 'O son of mine uncle, if thou soughtest my eye, I would tear it for thee from its eyelids, and perforce I cannot but aid thee to thy desire and aid her also to her desire; for she is whelmed in passion for thee even as thou for her.' Asked I, 'And what is the interpretation of her signs?' and Azizah answered, 'As for the putting her finger in her mouth (an action common in grief and regret: here the lady would show that she sighs for union with her beloved), it showed that thou art to her as her soul to her body and that she would bite into union with thee with her wisdom teeth. As for the kerchief, it betokeneth that her breath of life is bound up in thee. As for the placing of her two fingers on her bosom between her breasts, its explanation is that she saith: "The sight of thee may dispel my grief." For know, O my cousin, that she loveth thee and she trusteth in thee. This is my interpretation of her signs and, could I come and go at will, I would bring thee and her together in shortest time, and curtain you both with my skirt.' "

CHAPTER X
INDIAN MYTHOLOGY

THE various religions of India are conspicuous for the complexity of their rites and observances. Both in Hinduism proper and in Buddhism, the mythology is elaborate and obscure, and symbolic attitudes and gestures are features of great importance. These gestures are depicted with careful precision in images, bas-reliefs and paintings, and they are also adopted in various devotional practices. In more secular circumstances they may be incorporated within the symbolology of the dance, as will be described later.

One example can be taken from the Hindu polytheism. In an Indian picture reproduced by Moor,[1,2] Mahâdevâ Panchamukhî (or Siva) is depicted seated in symbolic attitude, attended by his consort Pârvatî and the infant Ganêça. The god is represented with five faces, surmounted by a sixth and smaller head, and with ten arms. Each hand is held in a significant posture. Thus, the limbs on the right side of the body, may be described as follows: (i) thumb and first finger in contact and touching the cheek; (ii) fingers lightly flexed, the forearm being fully pronated; (iii) (this is a left-hand limb transposed to the right side) the attitude is the mirror opposite of (ii); (iv) (the main upper limb)

[1] Moor, E., *The Hindu Pantheon.* London. 1810.
[2] Moor, A. P., *Plates Illustrating the Hindu Pantheon.* London. 1861.

the tips of the thumb and the first finger are in contact; (v) the fingers are adducted and extended while the thumb is fully flexed across the palm. Of the limbs arising from the left side of the body: (i) (the main upper limb) lies across the chest with the tip of thumb touching that of the index finger; (ii) the forefinger is raised in full extension, the other digits being flexed; (iii) the hand is making a fist; (iv) the thumb and forefinger are extended and directed upwards, the other fingers being slightly flexed; and (v) the hand is extended with the palm directed downwards. Although each of these attitudes certainly represents a particular attribute or idea, the exact significance is not fully known.

The foregoing description is given merely as an example of the characteristics of Indian iconology. Certain postures are also associated with other deities. Thus Viśvakarman, the architect of the universe, is always represented in a sitting attitude, with his legs perpendicular and holding the forefinger of one hand with the fingers of the other. Kali (or Pârvatî), the consort of Siva, is often depicted in dark colours. In one representation she is seen trampling on the body of her husband, indicating the triumph of eternity over time. She is furnished with four arms; one hand holds a sword; another a human head; one hand points downwards to show the destruction around her; and the fourth is raised, presaging the regeneration of nature at a new creation. Others interpret the last two postures as signs of blessing and of reassurance.

Vishnu (the Preserver and second member of the

Hindu trinity) is shown as a four-armed deity with each hand grasping a symbolic object: a club to punish the wrongdoer, a shell blown on ceremonial occasions, a discus or emblem of rule, and a lotus as the sign of creative force.

Certain postures are traditionally associated with some members of the Hindu pantheon and receive specific designations.[1] Thus associated with Vishnu there is the *abhaya* gesture where the hand is raised with the palm directed forward signifying "fear not." In the *varada* or "bestowing" attitude the hand is directed downwards, the palm still being turned forwards. The *katihasta* posture comprises the left hand cupped, and resting lightly on the left hip. The *simhakarna* or "lion's ear" gesture consists in apposition of the thumb to the end of the second finger. There is also the *chikshatana* pose, also called the *chinmudrā*, where the palm is held upwards and forwards as in the "fearlessness" gesture but with the tips of the thumb and first finger in contact. This gesture is commonly made by the *gurus* or teachers as they expound the doctrines of the Vedanta. In the *kataka* pose, the second and third fingers are flexed while the palm is held upwards and forwards. The *anantasayana* attitude shows the deity reclining on his right side upon a coiled serpent; the right hand supports the head while the left arm lies extended along the side of the body.

Siva, and also his wife Uma, are often depicted in the *sukhāsana* or "attitude of ease." Here the

---

[1] Coleman, C., *The Mythology of the Hindus*. London. 1832.

divinity squats with the left leg abducted at the hip and fully flexed at the knee, while the right leg is semiflexed so that the foot hangs down.

In Buddhism[1] we found not only a continuation of the idea of ritual poses, but also an attempt at rationalization. So important are these postures, that under the term *āsana*, they rank as one of the eight requisites of Yoga, or Union with the Supreme Spirit of the Cosmos. Their efficacy is said to lie in the production of bodily relaxation. In the *padmāsana* or "lotus posture," for instance, the legs are folded under the body with the right foot placed on the left thigh and the left upon the right thigh. The *simhāsana* or "lion posture" is assumed by lying on the right side with legs extended and head supported by the right hand. Such was the attitude adopted by the dying Buddha, or "Lion." Other symbolic poses are found in the *virāsana* ("heroic posture"), the *kārmāsana* ("tortoise" posture), *kukkutāsana* ("cook" posture), *dhanur-āsana*, ("bow" posture). Ritual attitudes of the hands and fingers are known by the term *mudrā*, or "seal." They are to be regarded as the physical presentment of some *mantra* or magic formula, which is first generated in the mind and then uttered in speech. According to Campbell,[2] the formula or *mantra* is composed of Vedic texts; of the names of benevolent or malefic beings, preceded and terminated by "words of power"; or by a series of rapidly repeated nonsense-syllables.

---

[1] Monier-Williams, M., *Buddhism*. London. 1889.
[2] Campbell, A. J. D., Introduction to de Kleen's *Mudrās*.

The exercises or *āsanas* carried out by a Yogin have been described in more detail by Kuvalayananda.[1] Some of the postures are grotesque and require many months of practice before they can be correctly executed. It is claimed that each *āsana* is endowed with specific and powerful therapeutic efficacy, and it is indubitable that the Yogin, in the course of his exercises, contrives to effect an astonishing degree of voluntary control over the autonomic nervous system.

Combinations of *āsana* and *mudrā* are often to be seen in graven images of the Buddha. These attitudes have been classified into the sedent, the erect, and the recumbent. The first sedent attitude is known as the "meditative" or *dhyāna* posture. The Gautama's legs are in the lotus posture, while the supinated forearms lie in the lap so that the back of the right hand rests in the palm of the left. Another common posture is the "witness" or "earth-witness" attitude, or *bhumisparsa*. Here the right hand has moved from the meditative pose and, with the first two fingers, points downwards. Tradition tells that while in contemplation the evil Mara tempted the Gautama, who was about to attain Buddhahood. In reply to the taunt "who will bear witness for you?" the master pointed downward, saying: "Here is my witness"; immediately there rose an earth-spirit. Another pose is known as *tarka*—the "argumentative" or "teaching" attitude. Here the thumb and forefinger of the right hand are in contact with

---

[1] Kuvalayanda, *Asanas*, part i. *Popular Yoga*, vol. i. Lonavla, India; quoted by K. T. Behanan. *Yoga, A Scientific Evaluation*. London. 1938.

the finger-tips of the left. In the "preaching" attitude, the Buddha has raised the forefinger. The "benedictive" posture (*āsirvada*) is represented by the raising of the right hand. A rarer posture is an erect one known as the "mendicant" where the Buddha holds a bowl in one hand and screens it with the other. Images of the Maitreya Bodhisattva often show both hands raised, with the fingers in the lotus-shaped *mudrā*.

Some of these *āsana* can be seen in images pertaining to the Jain sect of Hinduism, as for instance in their figures of the Tirthakara, or perfected saints.

For various historical and ethnic reasons, the two great Indian religions of Hinduism and Buddhism have survived in the island of Bali so that the ritual gestures have been preserved in an unusually pure state. We owe to this fact the remarkable study of Miss De Kleen[1] on the subject. Visiting Bali first in 1920 for the purpose of studying the ritual gestures, she returned to investigate and record with her brush the *mudrā*-system employed by the *pedandas* or priests. These belong partly to the worship of Buddha and partly to that of Siva, though in Bali the differences between the two religious executants is not fundamental. According to the author the ceremony of prayer and *mudrās* takes place each morning, the priest being seated cross-legged facing the east. Head, body and legs remain immobile; the eyes are half closed. Passages from the *Vedas* are intoned, and also various magical formulae

[1] De Kleen, T., *Mudrās*. London. 1924.

(*mantras*) each one being accompanied by the appropriate *mudrā*.

The ritual includes the use of certain sacred articles, such as the rosary, bell, thunderbolt-sceptre, holy water, censer and lamp, which are held in significant hand-grips. In many of the *mudrās* a lotus-flower is held between the fingers, and the petals afterwards scattered towards the four points of the compass.

De Kleen made a collection of water-colour sketches of these *mudrās*, which were exhibited in 1923 at the Victoria and Albert Museum. Some of the interlacing postures of the fingers and hands are so intricate as to baffle verbal description. A record of one or two of the simpler may be given in illustration:

In the *mudrā* known as *ngili-atma*, the priest takes a flower between his two hands, touches his stomach with it, then describing a semi-circle before him, places the bloom in his hair. This act symbolizes the removal of the soul (or flower) from the stomach (where it normally resides in man) to the head (wherein the soul of Siva is located). After this identification of the priest with his God, the flower is removed from the hair to the stomach and then thrown away. The priest has become a man again.

In the *tatkarasodhana mudrā* the priest rubs along each finger, repeating a different formula over each. This action symbolizes the driving-out of impurity through the finger-tips.

In the *musti mudrā* the thumb and fingers of the

right hand are joined in a cone-shaped manner and then are held with the palm of the left hand, the thumb of which is abducted and extended. To the Buddhist this pose represents the union of male and female principles; to the Sivaist the gesture means the *Trimurti* or trinity of Brahmā, Vishnu and Siva.

The literature contains very little data concerning these symbolic attitudes. Hand-gestures employed by the priests of the Shingon sect of Japan were studied at the end of the last century.[1]

---

[1] Si-do-in-dzon, *Gestes de l'officiant dans les cérémonies mystiques des sectes Tendai et Singon (Bouddhisme japonais)*. D'après le commentaire de M. Horiose Toki, supérieur du temple de Mitrani-dji. Avec annotation et introduction par L. de Milloué, conservateur du Musée Guimes. Paris. 1899.

CHAPTER XI

OCCUPATIONAL SIGN-LANGUAGES; DIGITAL METHODS OF COUNTING

There are also private sign-languages practised by members of many trades and professions. Various reasons are found for the use of such codes; the noise of the environment may preclude conversation; or barter may be carried on between peoples who speak different languages; or secrecy may be imperative; or deals may be in transaction between parties who are out of earshot, though within sight of each other. As examples of such professional sign-languages one can instance the dumbshow carried out by operatives in a noisy cotton-mill. The opposite state of affairs obtains in a broadcasting studio where silence and not noise necessitates the use of sign-talk. We may also instance the arm movements of the orchestral conductor which not only direct the tempo or rhythm, but also determine the expression with which the music should be played. Dumbshow is regularly used by traders in their barterings with savages, and this fact is well shown in the records of early voyages of exploration. Secrecy demands the use of signs rather than words between confederates in diamond transactions. We recall, too, the tictac men on the racecourse, one of whom takes up a prominent stand midway between the outer bookmakers and the enclosure. His business is to signal the starting-prices and to lay bets for his principal.

A confederate also forms an integral part in the "blower" system, and communicates with a watcher who is connected by telephone with a city office. In auction sale-rooms bids may be offered and accepted in dumbshow. Thieves, tramps, gypsies, prostitutes, drug addicts, practising sexual inverts also employ gesture at times to reveal their identity or to communicate with others of their kind.

Data interpreting some of these professional sign-languages is, of course, difficult if not impossible to secure.[1]

One may refer at this point to the gestures employed by children in the course of their play. Thompson Seton[2] has reckoned that in their games, American school-children make use of nearly one hundred and fifty different signs. Some of the well-known gestures are of course of considerable antiquity and symbolic significance. Thus the familiar rude gesture of the cocksnook, where the thumb is placed on the nose and the fingers spread, is a universal and age-old offensive sign. When children cross their fingers to secure a kind of armistice, they are probably executing an attenuated form of the Sign of the Cross.

Methods of counting upon the fingers have been known and practised since the Greeks. Numa Pompilius made use of such a system, as described

---

[1] Bishop Wilkins (*loc. cit.*) pointed out that secret signs should be inconspicuous and that common actions might be utilized as signals, for instance, scratching the head, rubbing parts of the face, winking the eyes, twisting the beard. "In which art," he said, "if our gaming cheats, and popish miracle-impostors, were but well versed, it might much advantage them, in their cozening trade of life."

[2] Seton, Ernest Thompson, *loc. cit.*

and illustrated in Abate (1797). We also find references to this manual arithmetic in Seneca, Tertullian, Martian Capella, the younger Pliny, St. Augustine, Orontes, Quintilian, Apuleius. Recent studies upon this subject have been made by Goldziher[1] and by Lemoine.[2]

The usual practice was to reckon on the left hand up to hundred, and thence to pass to the right hand. Perhaps this type of numerology was in Solomon's mind when he said, "Wisdom cometh with length of days upon her right hand" (Proverbs iii, 16)—meaning, it is suggested, that wisdom should make them live long, even a hundred years. Bulwer[3] pointed out that arithmetical manual gestures are seen in various statues and monuments. Thus the two-faced image of Janus, Patron of Time and Ages, shows the fingers of the hands in an attitude which indicates the figure 365.

Interesting pictorial records of these hand-signs for numbers are to be seen in Bulwer's *Chirologia*. Still greater detail is contained in an older treatise[4] which has been incorrectly ascribed to the Venerable Bede.

Tylor, in his *Primitive Culture*, devotes a chapter to the art of counting. He discusses the manual methods of reckoning among various primitive races.

---

[1] Goldziher, I, *Zeit. d. Völkerpsychol. u. Sprachwissenschaft.* 16. 383.
[2] Lemoine, J. G., *Rev. des études islamiques.* 1932. 1. 1.
[3] Bulwer., *loc. cit.*
[4] "De loquela per gestum digitorum et temporum ratione," contained in Migne's *Patrologiæ.* Tomus xc. Paris. 1850 (col. 685 *et seq.*). (The Rev. Dom Gregory Dix, O.S.B., kindly informs me that this essay is often included among collected works of the Venerable Bede, but without justification.)

Most aborigines are unable to cope with an idea of numerals beyond three or four, and often their language gives a name to the first few numbers only. Thereafter, digital counting is employed. Thus the Bororos of Brazil, according to Martius, reckon 1, *couai*; 2, *macouai*; 3, *ouai*, and afterwards they count on their fingers, repeating the word *ouai*. When natives of Kamchatka were asked to count, they totted up all their fingers, then their toes, and having attained the figure twenty, asked what they were next to do (Kracheninnikow). The South American savages accompany the verbal utterance of numerals with manual signs; thus when they say "three" they at the same time hold up three fingers; or the whole hand in the case of the number "five" (Father Gumilla).

As evidence of the growth of verbal language out of gesture, Tylor mentions that in many savage societies such as the Tamanacs on the Orinoco, the Greenlanders, and the ancient Aztecs, the word for "5" is the same as for "hand"; "10" is the same as "two hands" or "half a man." The word "foot" corresponds with "15" and the numeral "20" is described by a word which indicates the joining together of hands and feet, or "one man." The Zulu language (Schreuder, Döhne, Grout) illustrates in a slightly different manner this metaphor of counting the fingers of the left hand, then the right, and then the toes. Their word for "5" is *edesanta* or "finish hand"; the Zulu then indicates the thumb of the right hand which he calls *tatisitupa*, or "taking the thumb" or "figure 6." The next numeral "7" is *kemba*, "to point," meaning the forefinger or "pointer." Figure "8" is *kijangalobili* or "keep back two fingers," while "9" is *kijangalalunje*, or "keep back one finger." *Kumi* means "10," and as each ten is completed the two hands are clapped together.

It has been said, also, that gypsies are unable to multiply beyond the figure 5, and therefore employ their fingers for all sums beyond. They assign a number to each finger of the two hands; the thumbs are 6, the index fingers 7, the second fingers 8, the ring fingers 9, and the little fingers 10. Multiplication is then carried out as follows: if it is desired to determine 7 times 8, the tip of the left forefinger (= 7) is placed against the tip of the second finger of the right hand (= 8). The two joined fingers and every finger beneath counts as 10. (In this case it will be both thumbs, both index fingers and one second finger; that is, 50 altogether.) The remaining fingers are then multiplied, i.e. two on the right hand and three on the left. The product, 6, is then added to the 50, giving the final product of 7 by 8.

CHAPTER XII

SIGN-LANGUAGE AND SYMBOLISM

THERE is a sign-language of symbolism, universal in its extent, and with its beginnings in the era of pre-history. We are well aware that certain gestures, known to ancient Egypt and Babylon, are in use to-day (Lutz[1]). Only that which mainly concerns the hand need, however, be discussed here. This system of gesture has, to some extent, passed into common currency, lying within the sphere of recognition of mankind in general. Other symbolic signs, although clear in their meaning, belong more to the domain of art, the theatre, heraldry and religion. Again there are others which are of universal though esoteric significance, comprehended by none but the initiated. Many signs, indeed, bear more than one interpretation; an obvious one—recognizable by all, and an occult one appreciated only by the few. It is interesting to note that the manual signs available for study are relatively few; and in the case of esoteric signs, it is significant that the hidden meaning usually remains constant, irrespective of time, place, and circumstance. In other words they cannot rightly be regarded as exclusive to any one system of occult thought, teaching, discipline or religion, but are the property of the common unconscious mind of mankind.[2-4]

[1] Lutz, H. F., *Osiris*. 1936. 2. 1. [2] Elworthy, F. T., *Horns of Honour*. London. 1900. [3] Elworthy, F. T., *The Evil Eye*. London. 1895.
[4] Bayley, H., *The Lost Language of Symbolism*. 2 vols. London. 1912.

The upraised hand, thumb and fingers together, is one of the commonest symbols. Frequently it is used as an emblem of power, authority or justice. It is the gesture made by a Jew on taking the oath in a law-court, and also by the newly elected President of the United States on assuming office. This symbol was often placed over the lintel of doorways in Spain and North Africa; it was familiar as the standard of the Roman legions. In heraldry, the arms of every knight baronet in the United Kingdom comprise an augmentation of a human hand gules, borne on an escutcheon in the centre or chief of the shield. As an amulet its usual object is to avert the evil eye, and for this reason it is often seen as a brass ornament upon the harness of cart-horses. Among the North American Indians a hand indicates a prayer to the Great Spirit or Master of Life; in their picture-writing, its meaning is power, strength, mastery. During the first eight centuries of Christianity, a hand was the symbol of God the Father, a conception borrowed from older religions. (The Roman Church carries the symbolization still further, and associates the thumb with God the Father, the third finger with Christ the Son and the second finger with the Holy Ghost. Two fingers placed upon the palm signify the divine and the human nature of Christ.) In India a golden hand is the sign of labour and of the productive power of the sun. It constitutes a common gesture depicted in statues of Vishnu, and here it signifies reassurance. The raised hand is also at times a symbol of adoration or blessing and as such is seen in medieval paintings of the Virgin at the Annunciation.

The left hand was used by the devotees of the cult of Isis as a symbol of justice. In the second century, Apuleius,[1] who was initiated into the Eleusinian mysteries, described one of the grand ceremonies. We read in his account . . . "the fourth (i.e. performer in the ceremony) displayed the emblem of Justice, the figure of the left hand with the palm open, which, on account of its natural inactivity, and its being endowed with neither skill nor cunning, has been judged a more fitting emblem of justice than the right." This manual emblem was also known to the Gnostics, and it has been associated with the Brahmin *argha* or *yoni*, and hence a symbol of the passive power of nature.

An upraised hand, fashioned in brass with a heart piercing the palm, is an emblem often borrowed by Friendly Societies, for its meaning is "fidelity to charity."

A hand closed except for the first two fingers, which remain extended (together or apart) also represents, at times, justice. When the Regent of Hungary protested against the injustice of the Treaty of Trianon, he accompanied the words *Nem nem, soha!* (no, no, never) with this gesture. A bronze reproduction of this hand-sign has been set up in the Square of Victory in Budapest. Hands in this attitude were often made of wood or clay, and encircled with a serpent; ancient Romans placed

---

[1] Apuleius, L., *The Golden Asse*. (Aldington's translation, 1566). Book XI.

these in their homes possibly as votive offerings. The same hand-posture, turned upwards, is a sign of blessing (*Mano pantea*). Such a gesture can be made only by one high in ecclesiastical rank. It survives in the papal blessing, and it is the mode of benediction favoured by medieval artists in their representations of the Deity. In the Orthodox church, the fourth finger is also raised in the act of benediction so that the third finger alone is bent.

One of the oldest symbolic hand gestures is one in which the fingers are closed into a fist, except the first and the fourth, which remain in full extension. This gesture is described as the *manu cornuta* or "the horns"; it was in common use in ancient Rome and it is well known to-day to all Italians and other Mediterranean peoples. It is seen in paintings and images in Burma, India, Ceylon and Japan. A Moslem places his hand in this posture while reciting the Creed. Held vertically this gesture represents love; horizontally, justice. But the usual meaning attached to this gesture is protection against the evil eye. The gesture is then made with the extended fingers directed towards the offending person. Until recently this device of a *manu cornuta* could often be seen as an amulet worn by Italian children. To students of esoteric religion the two outstretched fingers represent the horns of Isis and of Diana. A gesture made with the hand in this posture may also have a subsidiary meaning, namely a suggestion of cuckoldism or marital infidelity (Knight[1]).

An even stronger hand-sign against the evil eye

---

[1] Knight, R. Payne, *loc. cit.*

is made with the fist lightly closed, and the thumb inserted between the first and second fingers. This is known as the *mano in fica,* or the "fig." This sign is full of contumacious obscenity, for the fig is a world-wide sexual symbol. The *mano in fica* is a gesture of vulgar abuse and often carries a further implication of effeminacy or dubious virility. This symbol is at the basis of such expressions as *far la fica*; *faire la figue*; "I don't give a fig." Emblems of a hand in this attitude were frequently associated with the phallus, and the two symbols were carried together in ceremonial processions. Ovid spoke of this gesture as the *manus obscaena.* To-day the hand serves as an amulet, sold in Mediterranean countries as a charm against the evil eye; or, as in Batavia, as a cure for sterility.

The "fig" is thought by some to be seen in a different form in the gesture of putting the thumb or finger into the corner of the mouth and drawing it down, as found among the relics of Herculaneum. The meanings of the two symbols are very similar; it is probable that Shakespeare's allusion to "biting the thumb" refers to this gesture.

Other hand signs and symbolic meanings may be mentioned briefly. The third or ring finger is sometimes termed the *digitus medicus* being used in the practice of healing or "striking" in the middle ages.[1] Placing the palms together is well-known as an attitude of devotion, but in the Neapolitan gesture-talk a slight modification of this becomes a mark of

---

[1] According to early Latin tracts, the five fingers are to be designated as *pollex, index, impudicus, medicus* and *auricularis.*

stupidity. Clasping of the hands is a familiar emblem of "brotherly love." A gesture made by placing together the tips of the thumb and of the first finger is widely employed, particularly in Hindu and Buddhist mythology. It is also used during the Roman Mass in the act of blessing.

The extended thumb is widely employed as a gesture meaning "good" (thumbs up) or simply as an affirmation. We are familiar with this sign in Roman times during gladiatorial contests. The same gesture is made by mendicant Lhamas in Tibet while begging. Moslems employ this sign during their circumcision rites. In Roman Catholic practice the thumb serves in the rites of baptism and of anointing.

In addition to the foregoing, there are a number of manual postures of equally widespread significance rich in symbolic content. These gestures have been spoken of by Ward[1] as "mantric signs" in that they are, as it were, prayers in themselves; comparable with the offering-up of prayers in a dead and unfamiliar tongue. Of these numerous mantric signs may be mentioned, quite shortly, the signs of preservation; of distress; of fidelity; of sacrifice; of horror; of destruction; of blessing; and many others. Ward, who has devoted considerable attention to this subject, reports that these mantric signs have been observed in almost every form of pictorial art, on almost every material, just as they are to be found in every age and every clime. In his monograph,

[1] Ward, J. S. M., *The Sign Language of the Mysteries*. 2 vols. London. 1928.

he has described these signs occurring in Egyptian papyri; engraved in stone and bronze; on seals; in terracotta figurines; on a gold ring from Mycenae; on Greek painted vases; a Carthagenian lamp; on ivory carvings; illuminated manuscripts; Cloisonne enamels and monumental brasses; pictures; tiles; stained glass; shields, native beads; woven hangings; funeral vases in the New World. Ward emphasizes that these signs are utilized to-day in primitive rites of initiation and in secret brotherhoods. He explains that a knowledge of symbolic art is only possible through an understanding of the inner meaning of the ancient sign-language, "which has been handed down from generation to generation, usually under the protection of religion, and is still in use to-day in every quarter of the world."

CHAPTER XIII

GESTURE IN CONVERSATION: THE NEAPOLITANS AND THE LEVANTINES

Gesture has already been defined as the movements accompanying speech serving the purpose of emphasis. They may embellish the flow of talk when purely propositional qualities are involved; or they may adorn speech which is heavily charged with feeling-tone. In the transition from quiet conversation to declamation and from thence to rhetoric, the play of gesture usually increases. Gestures serve to decorate the subject-matter of speech like illustrations in a book; so too, the abuse of gesture may defeat its purpose by distracting the attention away from the theme.

Montaigne[1] was aware of the value of signs in speech, pointing out that they were understandable by animals and by children. To illustrate the utility of gesture he proceeds . . . "And why not, as well as our dumbe men dispute, argue and tell histories by signes? I have seene some so ready and so excellent in it, that (in good sooth) they wanted nothing to have their meaning perfectly understood. Doe we not daily see lovers with the lookes and rowling of their eyes, plainly shew when they are angrie or pleased, and how they entreat and thanke one another, assigne meetings, and expresse any passion?

E'l silentio ancor suole
Haver prieghi et parole.

[1] Montaigne, *loc. cit.*

> Silence also hath a way,
> Words and prayers to convay.

"What doe we with our hands? Doe we not sue and entreat, promise and performe, call men unto us and discharge them, bid them farewell and be gone, threaten, pray, beseech, deny, refuse, demand, admire, number, confesse, repent, feare, bee ashamed, doubt, instruct, command, incite, encourage, sweare, witnesse, accuse, condemne, absolve, injurie, despise, defie, despight, flatter, applaud, blesse, humble, mocke, reconcile, recommend, exalt, shew gladness, rejoyce, complaine, waile, sorrow, discomfort, dispaire, cry out, forbid, declare silence and astonishment? And what not? With so great variation, and amplifying, as if they would contend with the tongue. And with our head, doe we not invite and call to us, discharge and send away, avow, disavow, belie, welcome, honour, worship, disdaine, demand, direct, rejoyce, affirme, deny, complaine, cherish, blandish, chide, yeeld, submit, brag, boast, threaten, exhort, warrant, assure, and enquire? What doe we with our eyelids? and with our shoulders? To conclude, there is no motion, nor jesture that doth not speake, and speakes in a language very easie, and without any teaching to be understood; nay, which is more, it is a language common and publike to all: whereby it followeth (seeing the varietie, and severall use it hath from others) that this must rather be deemed the proper and peculiar speech of humane nature."

The same idea was expressed centuries earlier by Quintilian ... "The action of the other parts of the body assists the speaker, but the hands (I could almost say) speak themselves. By them do we not demand, promise, call, dismiss, threaten, supplicate, express abhorrence and terror, question and deny? Do we not by them express joy and sorrow, doubt, confession, repentance, measure quantity, number and time? Do they not also encourage, plead, restrain, convict, admire, respect? and in pointing out places and persons, do they not discharge the office of adverbs and of pronouns?"

Individuals differ widely in their habit of gesture. In this connection there are many factors which may be of importance, such as bodily and mental constitution, and of course race. Mediterranean peoples are notorious for their propensity for gesture, and can be contrasted with the more static Nordic peoples and also with such far Eastern races as the Chinese. Addison in the eighteenth century contended that gesture did not suit the genius of the Englishman, even in rhetorical utterance. There is to some extent a direct connection between volubility and the use of gesture. It is not improbable, too, that scholarship is a factor, for as people read more and write more they tend to speak in conformity with literary standards and to employ gesture but little. Hence it would be anticipated that gesture might be elaborate in communities where there is a marked distinction between spoken and written language; one would therefore expect to find the Turks and the Chinese employing gesture a great deal, but such is not the case.

The question of tradition and instruction is most

important though often overlooked. Many systems of training seek to obliterate any undue evidences of emotional drive during speech, and under this discipline gesture too becomes inhibited. Thus most educated Nordic people are taught to restrain tendencies towards gesture and emotional display of all kinds. Indeed in some very rigid educational systems —as among the Samurai of Japan—the proscription refers chiefly to any betrayal of emotion which might be displeasing or painful to others; thus a Japanese is taught to receive unpleasant news with a blandly smiling countenance.

Of all the peoples who make use of gesture in profusion, the Neapolitans and the Sicilians are preeminent. It is possible that they have directly inherited some of the traditions of the theatre from their Greek, Roman and Carthaginian ancestors.

It has been said that the use of gesture of Sicily dates from the dictatorship of Hiero, who prohibited public meetings; sign-language was therefore thought to be the mode of evasion. This hypothesis scarcely accounts for the wide use of gesture along the whole Mediterranean littoral.

The astonishing repertory of facial and expressive movements which may embellish the declamations of Italians has been carefully documented by Rosa.[1] His monograph contains not only a precise description of such mimic movements, but also a collection of over three hundred beautiful illustrative plates. Neapolitan gestures have also been studied a little over a century ago by two eminent ecclesiastics; the

[1] Rosa, L. A., *Espressione e mimica*. Milan. 1929.

GESTURE IN CONVERSATION

Canon de Jorio[1] and Cardinal Newman.[2] The former drew up a detailed word-sign dictionary and furthermore augmented his data from the store of Italian art. The latter gave an entertaining description of an imaginary conversation between two Neapolitan gentlemen, explaining *seriatim* the various gestures.

Earnest remonstrance: the two palms are pressed together, the fingers close together, the thumbs depressed. The hands are then rhythmically moved up and down.

A more personal appeal: all the fingers and the thumb of the right hand are joined together and the united points are pressed upon the forehead.

Disappointment: striking the forehead.

Sincerity: pressing the region of the heart.

To-morrow: a semicircle is drawn in the air with the forefinger, from below upwards (? indicating the revolution of the sun).

Hunger, poverty: beating the ribs hard with the flat of the hand.

Suspicion: forefinger placed alongside the nose.

Deceit: fingers placed between the cravat and the neck, rubbing the neck slowly with the back of the hand.

Hunger: points of the thumb and forefinger applied around the mouth with rapid alternations in a vertical and in a horizontal direction (? indicating a sealing-up of the mouth).

Death, failure: sign of the cross made in the air.

Stupidity: thumb against temple; hand open.

Cunning: forefinger draining down the outer corner of the eye.

Crab-like or tortuous: little fingers of both hands are hooked together, and both hands are moved forwards in a zigzag fashion.

Hard work: rubbing the forehead with the thumb from side to side.

[1] de Jorio, A., *La Mimica degli antichi investigata nel gestire napolitano.* Naples. 1832.
[2] Newman. *Essays on Various Subjects,* vol. iii. London. 1853. (Reprinted from the *Dublin Review* for July 1837.)

Bribery: pinching the cheek between thumb and fingers and shaking the hand.
Avarice: clenched fists pressed against the chest ("close-fisted.")
Theft: fingers drawn in and closed in a hook-like manner.
Gambling: closing the left hand before the breast as if holding something tight between the thumb and forefinger and then drawing something with the right.

De Jorio and others believe that these Neapolitan signs are partly at least derived from the signs and gestures which formed part of the religion of ancient Rome and Greece. He insists that the frescoes and statues of antiquity bear in addition to their obvious meaning a *double entendre* which can be interpreted by a study of the attitude of the hands. Indeed some knowledge of the modern sign-language is necessary for the interpretation of these classical works of art. Many examples are given by de Jorio to support this contention. Both Newman and de Jorio refer to the significance of the hand gestures in the paintings of medieval Italy, and Newman mentions that a Neapolitan would find the hand-postures of the figures in say "The Last Supper," pregnant with hidden meanings.

The same abundance of gesture can still be found among the Levantines of to-day. It is interesting to observe that the signs are often identical with those of the Neapolitans and possess the same meaning. At other times the gestures and their significance are quite different.

Signs in common use in the Near East include:

No: a backward jerk of the head accompanied by a clicking noise made with the tongue. (This sign is of particular interest in that its meaning to the uninitiated would suggest affirmation rather than negation. In this way it forms an exception to the almost universal employment of nodding movements of the head to indicate "yes.")

"Not at all" or *"By no means":* the thumb is placed under the upper incisor teeth and is then rapidly flicked forwards. (This sign is also used in the South of France.)

Approval or *approbation:* stroking the chest downwards with the right hand two or three times. The ironical exclamation "Och! och" often accompanies this. Another sign is made by an apposition of the tips of all the fingers and the thumb of the right hand; the hand, with finger-tips directed upwards, is moved up and down a few times.

Disapproval: shaking the collar or coat lapel with the right hand.[1]

Theft or thief: the right hand is held down by the side; the hand is opened wide and then slowly all the fingers are brought together again.

Insulting gesture: the open hand is put against another person's face or held up before him, with the words "na, sta matia sou" (Greek: "On your eyes let it be.")

"He has disappeared" or *"it has gone":* opening the hand and blowing into it.

Anger: the little fingers are hooked together and then released. This manœuvre is repeated two or three times.

Provocation: The inner side of the right fist beats against the top of the outer side of the left fist. Turkish children, making this sign, at the same time cry "Bisko! Bisko!" meaning "I dare you!"

Disbelief: the index finger pulls down the lower lid of the left eye.

"Finished": the palm of one hand brushes the other.

Concord; agreement: the two index fingers, palmar surfaces down, are rubbed together.

Some of these gestures have also been mentioned by Lutz[2] as occurring among the Arabs.

Efron and Foley[3] have recently compared gestural

---

[1] This gesture was described, though with an incorrect interpretation, by Petermann in his *Reisen im Orient*, p. 172. [2] Lutz, H. F., *loc. cit.*

[3] Efron, D., and Foley, J. P., Jnr., *Zeit. f. Sozialforsch*. 1937. 6. 151. Quoted by A. Anastasi, *Differential Psychology*. New York. 1937.

behaviour of Italian and Jewish immigrants in New York. Their material was made up of three groups: (1) "traditional" Italians living in "Little Italy," New York City; (2) "traditional" Jews from the East Side ghetto, New York City; and (3) "assimilated" Italians and Jews living in "Americanized" environments. The Jews were mainly of Lithuanian or Polish stock, while most of the Italians were from Southern Italy or Sicily. Certain differences were noted between the gestural patterns of the Jews and of the Italians. The latter chiefly used the arms in gesticulating while the former also brought into play the head, hands and fingers. Italians made gestures which continued and ended without changing direction, while the movements among Jews were more sinuous and erratic. Simultaneous and symmetrical arm-movements characterized the Italians, while Jews tended to employ gestures which were unilateral or else asymmetrically bilateral. The range of the gesture-movements was wider among the Italians, and there was a tendency for the hand to wander far away from the median plane of the body. Italians made movements which were more often centrifugal in direction; Jews preferred centripetal gestures. The tempo of the movements was jerky and sporadic among the Jews. Their gesticulations were more of the discursive or logical type, portraying not only the object but also the process of ideation. The Italian gestures were more pictorial and pantomimic.

Amongst the "assimilated" groups of Jews and Italians, the play of gesture was far less evident, and racial distinctions were ill-defined. The differences in gestural behaviour between "traditional" and "assimilated" communities could not be ascribed to factors of "generation." Thus American-born students at an orthodox Jewish school made the same use of gesture as the ghetto dwellers, while American-born Jewish members of an exclusive Fifth Avenue club showed none of the characteristic expressive movements.

CHAPTER XIV
THE ART OF RHETORIC

QUIET conversation passes by gradual gradation into the category of the harangue and thence to oratory. With this transition the play of gesture becomes magnified. In rhetoric indeed the correct marshalling of ordered and restrained gesticulation constitutes an art in itself. The proper use of gesture constituted in the time of the Roman Empire an exact study. Our classical treatise on the subject is Quintilian's *Institutes of Oratory*, a prosy and rather dull monograph, in which a chapter is devoted to the use of gesture.

Quintilian[1] (A.D. 40-99) points out that animals interpret our movements rather than our words, and that at times gesture seems to transcend articulation as a means of expression . . . "if our gesture and looks are at variance with our speech; if we utter anything mournful with an air of cheerfulness or, assert anything with an air of denial, not only impressiveness is wanting to our words but even credibility."

He then deals with gesture-movements of various parts of the body. The author emphasizes the importance of gracefulness in each gesture, and he stresses that there is a right way and a wrong way of executing each movement. The speaker's face, he teaches, should always be turned in the same direction as the movement of the hand, except when

[1] Quintilian, M. F., *Institutes of Oratory*, book xi, chap. iii.

referring to matters which arouse disapproval or aversion. It is a fault to gesticulate with the head alone; or to nod unduly often. To toss the head to and fro, and to shake and whirl about the hair are the "gestures of frenzied inspiration," according to Quintilian. The author condemns excessive contraction of the facial muscles, offensive grimacing and movement of the lips. "To shrug or contract the shoulders is seldom becoming, but begets a mean, servile and knavish sort of gesture."

Hand movements in orators, according to Quintilian, should not be imitative, in this way differing from the gesticulation of pantomime actors. Gestures should pass from left to right, they should begin and end with the sense of the words. Some have ordained that there should be an interval of three words between each movement of the hand but Quintilian objects that such a rule is impossible to follow. Some compromise is desirable between too much and too little action ... "the hand should be neither too long inactive nor disturb the speech as is the practice of many orators by perpetual motion." The free play of gesture may sometimes be checked by deliberately wrapping the hands in the mantle. This observation is well shown in a statue of the orator Aeschines contained in the National Museum of Naples. It is also laid down that the hand should never be raised above the level of the eyes, or lowered below the breast.[1] A

[1] We are reminded here of Hamlet's advice to the players ... "do not saw the air too much with your hand thus ... suit the action to the word, the word to the action; with this special observance, that you o'erstep not the modesty of nature."

curious objection is also made to gestures with the left hand, except when made in association with the right.

Faults in attitude are enumerated, especially for the benefit of advocates pleading in the law courts. The orator should not push forwards his trunk, and should correct the position of his feet. While addressing the Court he should take but few steps and never turn his back upon the Judge. He may, however, draw back by degrees . . . "some speakers even leap back, an act in the highest degree ridiculous." Other histrionic tricks are mentioned and condemned, such as swaying from one side to the other, and too frequent stamping of the feet. Quintilian admits, however, that the latter device is occasionally justifiable, as at the beginning or the end of a special argument. It is permissible to lean a little towards the Judge while pleading, but to lurch over towards the advocates on the opposite benches is a breach of manners. . . . "And for a speaker to fall back among his friends and be supported in their arms, unless from real and evident fatigue, is foppish."

Cicero's lecture on public speaking dealt shortly with expressive movements.[1] He cautioned the orator against adopting histrionic tricks of gesture. . . . "the action of the hand should not be too affected, but should follow the words rather than, as it were, express them by mimicry; the arm should be considerably extended, as one of the weapons of oratory; stamping of the foot should be used only

---

[1] Cicero, M. T., *de Oratore*, book iii, lix.

in the most vehement efforts, at the commencement or conclusion."

In 1644 Bulwer[1] published his *Chirologia*, dealing with the "naturell language of the Hand, as it had the happiness to escape the curse at the Confusion of Babel." This book constitutes another manual of instruction in the art of gesticulation. The same advice is given as to the use and abuse of gestures, the faults of hypo- and hypermimia, and the proscription of the left hand alone. It is obvious that Bulwer was inspired directly by the precepts of Quintilian.

[1] Bulwer, *loc. cit.*

CHAPTER XV

THE ART OF MIMING AND THE DANCE

PANTOMIMIC and gesture movements reach their peak of attainment in the theatrical art, and more especially in the mime, or silent acting. Here are found the apogee of expressive movements, for two objects must be attained, comprehensibility and beauty. The player must express not only all the gamut of the emotions but also a wide range of ideas. At the same time the movements must be performed with such grace and artistry as to make them an instrument of aesthetic value. These necessities demand a very high standard of technical efficiency.

Nowadays the legitimate stage does not demand the same mimic perfection, because of the important role played by diction and elocution. In the ancient Roman and Greek theatre, in the Oriental dramas, and during the reign of the silent films, the art of mime was supreme.

It is probable that acting grew out of miming, which in turn developed from the dance. Each of these art-forms has since struck out independently though for a time their spheres of activity overlapped. Mantzius[1] relates the origins of the dance to the reflection of joyful emotions in a series of bodily movements. These activities become associated with religious practices, first as an expression

[1] Mantzius, K., *A History of Theatrical Art*, vol. i. London. 1903 (10 vols.). (See also G. Vuillier, *A History of Dancing*. London. 1898.)

of emotional fervour, and later as a symbol. Hence we find the dance incorporated at some time within every religious belief in the world. Later still, the scope of dancing widened so as to include animal-mimicry as well as erotic and warlike motifs. With an increasing elaboration, the dance slowly developed into the historical dumb-show, the earliest silent drama.

With the growth of the mime, the study of the technical aspect expanded to form what has been termed Chironomy. One of the best known, and at the same time earliest, works on this subject was by Lucian.[1] This essay will be referred to later, but one may quote here his views on the mental and physical qualifications of an artist in the mime ... "he must have memory, sensibility, shrewdness, rapidity of conception, tact and judgment; further, he must be a critic of poetry and song, capable of discerning good music and rejecting bad. For his body, I think I may take the canon of Polyclitus as my model. He must be perfectly proportioned, neither immoderately tall nor dwarfishly short; not too fleshy (a most unpromising quality in one of his profession) nor cadaverously thin." Lucian also points out that while other arts call upon only half of a man's powers, either the bodily or the mental, pantomime makes demands upon both. The artist's performance is as much an intellectual as a physical exercise.

Of modern technical monographs, perhaps the

[1] Lucian, *Peri Orcheseus*. Collected works. Oxford translation. Vol. ii.

clearest are those of Aubert,[1] and Mawer,[2] wherein theory and practice of miming are described in detail. Aubert classifies dramatic movements into five types, viz.:

1. *Action movements,* which are merely those which are essential for the performance of an act: dancing, walking, etc.
2. *Character movements:* these are the permanent features which distinguish the character, habits, and quality of an impersonation.
3. *Instinctive movements,* or spontaneous, involuntary actions which betray an emotion, a moral or physical sensation.
4. *Complementary movements:* these consist in the co-operation of the whole body in the meaning indicated by the chief movement so that this expression is given more force and harmony.
5. *Descriptive or speaking movements,* or voluntary, studied, constructed movements which aim at expressing a thought, need or wish; or at describing a person or an object; or at indicating a place of direction.

The first four of these are "necessary, spontaneous, inevitable." They are enacted and understood by all. "They are the basic elements of the language of Nature, because Nature herself teaches them to us." The fifth class, comprising the speaking or speaking movements, is not "natural," and constitutes a type of artificial language. We can see here an analogy with the sign-talk of deaf-mutes where the first four classes of movements correspond with the instinctive elements, while the fifth group comprises the more conventional or symbolical gestures.

[1] Aubert, C., *The Art of Pantomime.* London. (No date.)
[2] Mawer, I., *The Art of Mime.* London. 1932.

Aubert says that a complete dramatic expression entails the interplay of posture, facial expression and gesture. Characterizations consist mainly of postures; portrayal of emotion is effected chiefly by facial expression; descriptive or speaking action is largely made up of manual gesture.

If Aubert's terminology is compared with the classification suggested in Chapter I, it can be said that the first and fifth groups correspond with "pantomime," while the third includes both "gesture" and "physiognomy."

In this manual of acting, the author enumerates the attitudes and movements which can be effected by the various bodily segments. Thus Aubert's discussion of hand movements can be quoted in illustration. He divided them into three classes: (1) *indicative gestures*, which point out an object; (2) *descriptive gestures*, which measure or delineate an object; and (3) *active gestures*, which illustrate the action they sketch.

According to Aubert, acting should consist "always in attitudes; often in facial expressions; rarely in gesticulations." Again he warns the actor "make only movements that are absolutely necessary."

Silent drama is largely composed of a series of descriptive or speaking movements, and it is interesting to analyse these gestures from the standpoint of grammar. As in the sign-language of deaf-mutes, Indians and aborigines, certain grammatical forms and also ideas cannot be directly translated into pantomime and will need to be portrayed by the ruse of periphrasis. For example, pronouns of the third person can be expressed only when they apply to people actually present, while relative pronouns (others, such, some) can scarcely be enacted at all. Verbs constitute the unit of pantomimic action, and nouns are usually portrayed by way of their appropriate function. Thus "pen" is expressed in the mime by the action-verb "to write." Again, adjectives are usually interpreted by changing them into verbs of action or of feeling. Adverbs are enacted without great difficulty, except those of time which are impossible of expression. Articles, prepositions and conjunctions cannot be rendered by the actor's art. The enactment of verbs denoting past and future time is difficult, and the meaning can only be given by technical tricks in stagecraft. As an example Aubert takes the scene of a gentleman dressed for the ball returning home to be greeted by his wife with the remark: "While you were dancing there I was weeping here alone." The pantomimist would be forced to enact these lines, thus: "Out there—you dance—alone—here—I weep."

The weakness of the mimic art lies in the difficulty which narration meets as soon as action, or the dialogue of action, is abandoned. It becomes almost impossible to deal intelligibly with such situations as speaking of a person who has not yet appeared upon the scene or who is off stage, or of an object not on the stage, or retailing a past action or outlining a future one.

This analysis of the craft of silent acting shows

the great advantage which the deaf and dumb possess in their sign-talk. Whereas there are a number of grammatical forms difficult or impossible for the actor to portray, these may be well within the powers of the deaf-mute to execute and comprehend. Thus adverbs of time—which cannot be rendered intelligibly in the silent drama—are shown by the deaf and dumb in simple empirical gestures which, incomprehensible to the outside world, are at once recognized by the deaf.

In the ballet we encounter an off-shoot of the technique of miming. In this art-form the aesthetic factor is dominant and comprehensibility is of lesser importance. A simple theme is chosen, less for the sake of the story, than as a vehicle for an intricate sequence of graceful and significant movements. We therefore find a large number of stylized attitudes and gestures introduced, the interpretation of which is aesthetic rather than propositional. The aesthetic atmosphere is enhanced by the use of music which also supplies some measure of temporal control. Even within the sphere of the dance, we find aestheticism and acting varying in their proportions; ranging from such mainly mimic productions as *Thamar*, through stylized classical ballets like *Les Sylphides*, to those modern symbolic and largely idiosignificant themes exemplified in *Choreartium*.

CHAPTER XVI

THE GRAECO-ROMAN THEATRE

GESTURE was an important element in the stage-craft of the Greek drama. The chorus, a characteristic feature of this period, performed through various mediums—speech, dramatic recitation, singing, dancing. The dance (Orchesis) was a highly esteemed and important art, which, very closely associated with singing, also formed part of tragedy, comedy and the satires. Dancing implied far more than movements of the lower limbs. It included mimetic actions of the arms and body, as well as postures, illustrating and interpreting the poetry. Aristotle defined dancing as an imitation of actions, characters, and passions by means of postures and rhythmical movements. Plutarch divided dancing into motions, postures, and indications. Of these the first served to depict actions and emotions; postures were the attitudes in which the various motions were so to say crystallized; "indications" were gestures which merely pointed out persons or objects. Much of the dancing was relegated to the chorus. The *choreutai* wore cumbersome traditional masks, *kothornoi* (or high stilt-like shoes), padded breast-plates, and long trailing garments. In this way, their mobility was gravely hampered, and the miming was restricted to movements of the hands and arms. These were rendered in an expressive and picturesque a fashion as possible, and the proper training of such mimicry became as special and precise an art as that of modern dancing. During long speeches in the recitative the chorus did not remain immobile but enacted in dumb show the content of the actors' talk. Thus in the *Clouds*, while Strepsiades narrates his quarrel with Pheidippides, the *choreutai* mime the various incidents, keeping in strict time with the dialogue. Three modes of acting were known: speech adorned with gestures but unaccompanied by music; song, supported by dance and accompanied by the flute or the harp; and the melodramatic recitation or rhythmic declamation, with music and gesture in support, and at times also dancing. The dance varied in a traditional manner according to the type of drama. Tragedy was characterized by the solemn and stately *emmeleia*; thus when in the *Persae* Xerxes and the elders mournfully return to the palace, the *choreutai* rend their garments, pluck at their hair and beards, and strike their breasts and foreheads. The licentious *kordax* formed part of comedy. Here the movements were coarse, suggestive and unrestrained. The satires were supported by the grotesque *sikinnis* where the *choreutai* were naked except for a loincloth with phallus and tail attached. Here skipping and jumping movements were rapid and violent, and caricatured the noble and graceful gestures of tragedy (Haigh).[1]

In Greece, the dance also constituted an art of its own, independent of the drama. The four chief types of Greek dances were the Funeral, the Ritual,

[1] Haigh, A. E., *The Attic Theatre*. Third edition. Oxford. 1907.

the Vintage, and the Athletic. There were also the Dionysiac dances; the Pyrrhic dances wherein the Greek soldiery exercised their arts before combat; the devotional and processional "hymns;" the Dithyrambs; Prosodia; Parthenia; the Hormos or chain-dance; the Geranos, representing the escape from the Labyrinth; Epilenios, a dance of the wine-press; and the Pindaric Threnes and Hyporcheme. All agreed in utilizing symbolic gestures and attitudes in high degree, and these postures are easily recognized in the numerous vase-paintings which have come down to us.

The Roman theatre comprised both the mimes and the pantomimes. In the former men and women took part. The conventional attire of the Greek drama was abandoned and on this account the mimic actors were sometimes termed the *planipedes* or "flat-footed." A variety of coarse and riotous burlesques formed the main themes for the mimes, and distinguished contemporaries were often held up to ridicule. This type of entertainment was very popular with the lower classes.

The pantomimes conformed more to "interpretive dancing" (Nicoll) or what we usually understand to-day under our term "mime." They were essentially gesture-plays and they attained a high degree of popularity as well as a superlative pitch of technical skill. Tragedies, legends and mythological subjects were commonly chosen, such as Venus and Mars in the net of Vulcan, Leda and the Swan, Danae and the golden shower, Venus and Adonis, Apollo and Daphne. The Greek text was sung by a chorus or by a singer with cymbals fastened to the ankles to accentuate the rhythm. Costumes and masks were worn.

There were also the Salic or ritual dances carried out by the priests of Mars. After a procession through the streets, dancing and singing followed, accompanied by beating of their sacred shields with staves.

One of the best contemporary accounts of the Roman theatre is to be found in the writings of Lucian of Samosata (A.D. 120). In his essay on pantomime, he narrates an imaginary argument between Crato who decries the art, and Lycinus who eloquently defends it. The latter traces the history of dancing and carries the story back to the creation of the universe. Demetrius the Cynic was another who despised the pantomime as a mere appendage to flute and pipe and beating feet. The gesticulations were described as aimless nonsense, adding nothing to the action of the play; the public was hoodwinked by the silken robes, the gorgeous masks, the music, and the singing, which served to set off what in itself was nothing. Lucian tells us, however, that Demetrius was challenged by the leading pantomime artist of the day to reserve judgment until he had personally witnessed his performance, which he promised to go through without the help of music. Time-beaters, flutes and the chorus were ordered to keep silent while the actor, holding the stage alone, represented the loves of Ceres and Aphrodite, the sun, the craft of Hephaestus, the capture of the lovers in the act, the surrounding gods—each in turn, the blushes of Aphrodite and the appeals of Ceres. Demetrius is said to have capitulated with enthusiasm. . . . "Man!" he exclaimed, "this is not seeing, but hearing and seeing, both: 'tis as if your hands were tongues."

Lucian also narrates that a visiting member of the royal house of Pontus was taken by Nero to a pantomimic performance. Although the visitor could not fully understand the dialogue, he was greatly impressed by the intelligibility of the gestures. On his departure, Nero inquired what gift he would like to take back to Pontus and the visitor requested the pantomime artist, to serve as an interpreter at home among the many-tongued subjects and neighbours of the Pontine Kingdom.

Under the reign of Augustus the pantomime reached its peak. The names of some of the great exponents of the art have come down to us: Pylades, Bathyllus, Paris—the friend of Nero and lover of the Empress Domitia, Quintus Roscius, Mnestu the favourite of Caligula, Cleon, Hylas, Nymphodonus. Even Nero thought highly of himself as a pantomimist. The great actresses included Arbuscula, Lucilia, Tymele, Denisa, Cytheris. One, Theodora, also spoken of as "The Whore," became the wife of the Emperor Justinian. As evidence of the regard with which the pantomime artists were held, it can be recalled that during a famine a large number of city-dwellers were evacuated; three thousand dancers, however, were allowed to remain. Many became very wealthy; Aesopus, after a life of extravagance, left an estate of over £175,000, while Roscius received an income of about £4,350. Tiberius, indeed, had to put some check upon their social aspirations.

With the decline of Rome and the rise of Latin christianity, the pantomimes were ruthlessly persecuted and ultimately extinguished.

CHAPTER XVII
THE ORIENTAL THEATRE

In India, the drama and the dance are very closely associated, the same word *Nātya* signifying both arts. The stage-craft of the drama is so precise that the gestures are as fixed as a musical score. Nothing is left to chance and the actor will no more yield to impulse in a spontaneous gesture than in an interpolated line. Singers also accompany their art by movements which are as pre-determined as the melody.

In an Indian poem called Mâlavikâ we read of an actress's achievement: "All was blameless and in accordance with the rules of Art, for the meaning was completely expressed by her limbs, which were full of language; the movement of her feet was in perfect time, she exactly represented the sentiments."

There is a strong religious colouring to the Indian drama, and Siva was often depicted as Lord of the Dance. Bala Krishna was also frequently shown in a dancing pose. The ritual hand postures, or *mudrās*, of the Buddhists and Sivaists can be traced in the theatrical technique. Symbolism may be an integral part of both the secular and the hieratic performances. Thus each finger may be associated with its own colour, sound, element, and even its own celestial guardian.

With their characteristic love of classification and

indexing, the Indians divide up the vocabulary of gesture. Thus they recognize three chief kinds of gesture—bodily, vocal and ornamental. Bodily gestures are divisible into movements of the limbs, of the body, and of the features. Of head movements nine are detectable, though some authorities recognize twenty-four. Even the glances are made to fall into eight classes (forty-four classes according to some writers). There are six recognizable movements of the brows, and four of the neck. Twelve "lives" or hand-movements are demonstrable. Other authorities relegate manual gestures into single and combined movements, of which there are twenty-eight of the former and twenty-four of the latter. There are eleven hand movements indicative of relationship. Various gestures refer to the nature and deeds of the gods. There are gestures denoting the four castes. Furthermore hand movements are known which denote famous emperors, the lords of the earth, the seven oceans, well-known rivers, the upper and lower worlds, various trees, animals, birds and fishes (Nankikésvara).[1]

The same authority describes the numerous symbolic meanings which have been attached to each hand posture. Two examples may be given in illustration: In the *Bhramara* or "bee" attitude, the tip of the second finger touches that of the thumb; the forefinger is bent while the third and fourth fingers are extended. This gesture indicates a bee, parrot, crane, cuckoo, and also union. According to another

[1] *The Mirror of Gesture* (being the *Abhinaya darpana* of Nankikésvara). Translated by A. Coomaraswamy and G. K. Duggirala. Cambridge. 1917.

source, this gesture originates from Kaśyapa when he made earrings for the mother of Devas. Its sage is Kapila, its colour dark, its race Khacara, its patron saint the king of Flying Creatures. Its usage includes *Yoga* (union); vow of silence; horn; tusk of an elephant; picking flowers with long stalks; taking out a thorn; untying the girdle; adverbs of two letters; flying creatures; dark colour.

A more complicated bimanual gesture is known as *Udvestitâlapadma*. The hands, with fingers widely abducted and extended, are held across the chest with the palms upwards. Here the patron saint is Śakti. It signifies husband; humble words; the breasts; full-blown lotus; saying "I am beloved"; conversation; desire.

In Moslem countries gesture-play is encountered in the occasional religious dances. Thus the dancing dervishes of Galata, now expelled from republican Turkey, displayed frenzied movements of the trunk and limbs. The attitudes and postures were not executed haphazard but each was determined by as rigid a code of choreography as in a classical ballet.

Mimetic dances were popular in ancient Japan. In modern times miming plays an important part in the *kagura*, or song-dances with musical accompaniments. The traditional *Nō* plays of Japan[1] include the use of song, music, speech and miming. The tap or beat of the footsteps is conspicuous just as it was in the Greek or Roman theatre. The resemblance is further enhanced by the use of masks, the conventional but elaborate costumes, the absence

[1] Stopes, M., *Japanese Nō Plays*.

of scenery and properties, and the important role of the chorus.

In China, modern miming developed out of the drama. At the time of the T'ang Dynasty (A.D. 618–907) songs were introduced into plays as an added attraction; still later dancing was also included. Gradually the dancer changed into the present system of conventional gestures. Despite various modifications there is an unbroken tradition between the modern and the ancient dramatic craft. Everything about the Chinese theatre is simple, stylized and symbolic—costume, scenery, characterization, motifs, use of colour and of masks. At first the actors wore long sleeves, but later white silk cuffs from 18 to 24 inches in length were attached, the seams being left open. These were called "rippling-water sleeves" from the appearance given by the gesticulations of the players. Leading artists wore longer and more elaborate sleeves than those playing minor roles. Correct sleeve movements became a matter of the very greatest importance and a hallmark of histrionic skill. It was necessary to synchronize the sleeve movements with the music and every effort was made to ensure gracefulness and artistry. More than fifty kinds of sleeve movement were recognized, some among the more important being the turning, the aside, the concealing, the repulsing, the greeting, the addressing, the weeping, the resting, and so on.

Next in importance were movements of the hand. At least ten types of manual gesticulation were taught, being classified as follows: the open hand, the helpless hand, the hindering hand, the fighting fist, the yielding hands, the contemplative hand, the fencing hand, the swimming hands, as well as numerous gestures of pointing.

In like fashion, various stereotyped movements of the arms, of the legs, the feet and of the waist were scheduled. Movements with pheasant feathers were also recognized. In addition there were various symbolical and conventional actions, as for example, traditional ways of crossing a threshold, opening and closing a window, mounting or dismounting a horse, sitting, placing of guests, embarking, pointing out a view through a window, etc. (Zung).[1]

The words of Jacovleff[2] may be quoted: "How often have I not observed the sober and graceful manner with which an actor opens a non-existing door and steps into an imaginary shadow. His precise and supple movement finds complete expression in the logic of rhythm, the basis of all plastic art. There is nothing confused or hesitating—combats and rapid movements are under absolute control. Suddenly everything is transformed into a statuesque vision. Yet it is not a gesture arrested in full action. Rather it is the static stylization of action. But it does not give one the idea of a lifeless pose. Sometimes a hand, sometimes a finger, sometimes a movement of the eyes gives you the dramatic sense of the action. But all is ruled by the perfect laws of rhythm. The expression of the gestures, the opposition of the movements, the sense of their

---

[1] Zung, C. S. L., *Secrets of the Chinese Drama.* Shanghai. 1937.
[2] Jacovleff, A. and Tchou-Kia-Kien, *The Chinese Theatre.*

dynamic value, produce an impression only possible through the medium of an art which, by the accumulation of century-old traditions, has become a perfect craft." Mawer[1] says that the Chinese actor excels in the visualization and mimic description of such themes as a galloping horse, the flowing of a river, and the movement of the rider or an oarsman. Lin Yutang[2] has also described the importance and precision of gesture and miming in modern Chinese stage-craft. He tells us that even in ordinary polite intercourse, correct and graceful movement is carefully cultivated. The educated Chinese has his own studied method of entering a room, greeting the assembly, playing chess and so on. When displeased a Mandarin may abruptly fling his arms downwards so that the turned-up "horse-hoof" sleeves fall with an audible jerk; this is called *fohsiu* or "brushing one's sleeves and departing."

---

[1] Mawer, *loc. cit.*
[2] Lin Yutang, *The Importance of Living*. London. 1938.

CHAPTER XVIII
GESTURE AS A PRECURSOR OF SPEECH

A CONSIDERATION of the foregoing chapters suggests that gesture (in the widest sense) can be broadly divided into two main groups. In the first of these we may relegate those instances of symbolic, conventional or empirical gestures which, while full of meaning, yet require interpretation. Such gestures are utilized for obvious reasons by members of secret brotherhoods. Signs of this nature also form part of the language of religious symbolism, of mythology, and of folk-lore. Not infrequently two or even more meanings may be attached to a single gesture.

The second great group of gestures is composed of those signs which bear an obvious interpretation, age-old and universal. These "instinctive" gestures constitute a silent *lingua franca* within the comprehension of all, whatever the age, race, religion, social status, or mental and cultural level. Such gestures can easily cope with themes of an emotional nature, and also with a large range of simple propositions. Certain abstractions, and ideas relating to past or future time, are expressed with greater difficulty.

It is at times necessary to add to this second system of instinctive gestures a number of empirical signs belonging really to the first group of signs. In this way the vocabulary is brought up to standards of adequacy for daily use. Examples of such hybrid sign-languages are to be found in the gestural systems of the deaf and dumb.

Although the two groups of gestures—symbolic and instinctive—are of great antiquity, we must regard the latter as being more primitive and more fundamental than the former. For example we find instinctive gestures often falling within the sphere of comprehension of animals, of young children before the acquisition of speech, and of mental defectives.

The problem arises as to whether these gestures really are "instinctive" in character, or whether they are passed on from one to another by a process of imitation. Darwin[1] devoted considerable thought to this question. Such expressive movements of the face as are often included within the term "physiognomy" are of course innate just as they are involuntary. Furthermore they can be demonstrated in congenitally blind subjects. Whether such common expressive movements of the limbs and trunk as kissing and shrugging the shoulders are also to be regarded as innate, is less obvious. Darwin believed these were, for they are known to occur in very young children, in those born without vision, and in widely different races. Laura Bridgman, bereft of vision, hearing and articulate speech, used to shrug her shoulders and raise her eyebrows like other people, in appropriate circumstances. As to such other common gestures as nodding or shaking of the head as signs of affirmation and denial,

---

[1] Darwin, C., *The Expression of the Emotions in Man and Animals*. Second edition. London. 1889.

the evidence is doubtful. Certainly there is not a world-wide uniformity of employment in this connection.

The subject of animal speech has nowadays become a serious biological study and we no longer regard mankind as sharply severed from the brute beasts by the possession of a faculty of articulate speech. It is unquestionable that animals possess audible means of inter-communication. Of course the most articulate creatures are not necessarily the most intelligent, and we must not make the error of regarding a parrot's talking as comparable with speech. Articulate speech among animals has not yet been studied in great detail but we already have grounds for believing that it is more complex than popularly imagined. People who have devoted close attention to the habits and behaviour of a particular pet animal have testified to this. As Montaigne said, writing on speech in animals: . . . "We manifestly perceive, that there is a full and perfect communication amongst them, and that not only those of one same kinde understand one another, but even such as are of different kindes.

> Et mutae pecudes, et denique secla ferarum
> Dissimiles fuerunt voces variasque cluere
> Cum metus aut dolor est, aut cum gaudia gliscunt.
>
> Lucr. V. 1069.

> Whole heard's (though dumbe) of beasts, both wild and tame
> Use divers voices, diffrent sounds to frame,
> As joy, or griefe, or feare
> Upspringing passions beare.

By one kinde of barking of a Dogge, the Horse knoweth he is angrie, but another voice of his, he is nothing dismaid."

In Schwidetzky's monograph[1] we find considerable evidence as to the existence of an "inherited" type of speech among the primates. This is a vocabulary of sounds, rich in vowels but poor in consonants. Various inspiratory clicking noises occur, analagous to those which are found as audible gestures in human speech, and which are characteristic of the Hottentot languages. Schwidetzky also traces the history of the study of animal speech, starting with Pierquin de Gembloux (1796–1863) the first to compile a dictionary of animal-sounds. Boutan (1913) concluded that the sounds emitted by the gibbon constituted no more than a "pseudo-speech." Learned (1923–24) distinguished thirty-two separate words in the chattering of chimpanzee; while Fourness drew up a dictionary of "orang-utan." Studies have also been made of speech in cocks and hens (Schmidt); horses (von Maday, von Unruh); wolves (Pfungst); cats (Römer); lower mammals (Landois); and higher mammals (Huxley and Koch).

From the gestural standpoint, however, we may say that articulate sounds are only a minor aspect of their faculty of comprehension. Animals recognize each other's changes of emotional state by a combination of simple gesture and expressive movements, with a limited series of crude sounds. There is no need to particularize beyond a mere mention of such phenomena as arching of the back, wagging

[1] Schwidetzky, *Do You Speak Chimpanzee?* London. 1932.

or lashing of the tail, baring of the teeth, erection of the hair, hissing and spitting. In the same way animals instinctively recognize certain simple gesticulatory movements which we make in their presence. Furthermore, they learn by association to react to various articulate sounds, such as a word of command. This is of course a commonplace example of Pavlov's conditioned reflex, and it is arguable whether one is justified in speaking of a "comprehension" by animals of human utterance.

As far as the animal kingdom is concerned, therefore, we may say that gesture forms a most important component of "speech," adopting Schuchardt's definition of speech as the "communication of what is thought, felt or willed." Moreover, we can justifiably assert that whatever sounds are emitted by the animal belong to the category of interjections, or audible gestures of the phonatory musculature. We may conclude therefore that gestures, silent or vocal, are all-important in animal speech.

A study of the comprehension and development of speech in infants and very young children shows that the baby learns to react to a number of simple gestures and movements made by the mother; later it learns to associate certain sounds with certain gestures, sounds which later still it succeeds in imitating. The infant too may execute crude gesture-movements of its own, some of which are audible and participate in the beginnings of speech. Thus the "dada" uttered universally by the infant may probably be due to tongue movements provoked by the erupting upper incisor teeth.

Speech may fail entirely to develop in some mental defectives, but except in the very lowest grades of idiocy, recognition of gesture obtains. So long indeed as consciousness remains intact, there is usually, both in aments and in dements, some reaction to a threatening gesticulation.

While then it is clear that gesture is a primitive component of speech, it is not arguable thereby that it is the forerunner of speech. Indeed we find throughout the vertebrate series, a parallelism between the development of gesture and that of audible speech. With the attainment of prehensile forelimbs, manual gesture became possible, reaching its peak of elaboration in men. Thus we find Aristotle describing man as the most mime-making of all animals. On the whole it is true to assert, moreover, that even amongst mankind the most voluble are also the most addicted to gesture. The two faculties, that of speech and that of gesture, seem to have developed side by side, gesture being comparable with an elder brother of speech.

We may therefore justifiably query the conclusion of some philologists that "the earliest human language may be said to have been a language of gesture signs." Swedenborg's phantasy that primitive man spoke a silent language of "internal respiration" or signs, must be considered unlikely.[1] At the same time we can scarcely doubt that primitive gestures were the immediate precursor of written language. The pictorial writing of the Aztecs, the Egyptians and the Chinese, has been

[1] Swedenborg, *Arcana Coelestia*. 1749–56.

clearly shown to be directly engendered by the mimic ideagrams of primitive peoples. Garrick Mallery, for instance, has demonstrated that the Indian manual signs for no, child, man, drink, water, tears, night are to be traced in an abbreviated or stylized form in the Maya, Egyptian, and Chinese characters representing these same ideas. Leibnitz indeed said that the writing of the Chinese might have been invented by a deaf person, though he also had in mind the peculiar syntax of the two languages.

Gesture possesses certain advantages over articulate speech; many of these have already been described when the deaf and dumb pantomime was discussed. Instinctive gestures are, in the first place, international and comprehensible to all whatever their language. They can be executed more rapidly than speech. They can express shades of meaning which could only be described by a circumlocution, and a modification of the main gesture can introduce adjectivally the idea of size, shape, speed, approval or disapproval and so on. Lastly there are a few propositions which can be expressed in words only with the utmost difficulty, but which can be explained instantaneously by means of a gesture. The word "spiral" is a striking example of a concept difficult to define but easy to demonstrate manually.

It seems therefore that gesture should be regarded as a very important modality of language, with origins at least as remote, and with great powers of enriching and enhancing our speech. Can any further development be expected or be usefully encouraged?

Paget[1] has estimated that it is possible to produce, by combining various postures, movements of the upper arm, forearm, wrist and fingers, no fewer than 700,000 distinct elementary signs. In this way the human hand can be regarded as 20,000 times as versatile as the mouth. It follows that great potentialities exist for the further development of gestural speech. He has therefore experimented with the idea of forming a universal sign-language based upon the use of Ogden's basic English. The dictionary of basic words contains only 850 items; Paget considers that something like 500 to 600 signs would suffice for the New Sign Language vocabulary.

Paget and his associates made a few preliminary conventions. The left forearm and hand, back up and fingers pointing forwards, held horizontally with the elbow touching the side is the general sign for *Time*. The same sign, but with palm up, means *Place*. A similar sign with the right hand, palm up, means *Thing*; with the back up it means *Abstract Idea*. Notions of time and of travel are made by modifications of the time and place gesture respectively.

It is not necessary to specify other examples taken from the New Sign Language but it is sufficient to say that a praiseworthy attempt is made to construct a logical system of simple gestures.

Gestures, like speech, may therefore be regarded

[1] Paget, Sir Richard, Paper read at the Royal Institute of Great Britain. 13, xii, 35.

as a dynamic and living subject which has not achieved finality in respect of development. A study of this aspect of language has served to indicate its fundamental nature and complexity. Lord Bacon was wise when he recommended as a subject of research for future generations "The Doctrine of Gesture or the Motions of the Body with a view to their Interpretation."

INDEX

Abraham, E. J. D., 24, 38
Addison, 87
Aeschines, 95
Allport, G. W. and Vernon, P. E., 14
Animal speech, 118, 119, 120
Aphasia, gesture in cases of, 25, 26, 27
— in a deaf-mute, 29
Apuleius, L., 80
Arabian Nights Entertainments, 62, 63, 64
Asana, 68, 69, 70
Asemasia, 28
Aubert, C., 100, 101, 102
Aungier, G. J., 52
Australian aborigines, sign-language among, 46–50

Bacon, Lord, 124
Bali, 70, 71
Ballet, the, 103
Basic English, 123
Bayley, H., 78
Bede, the Venerable, 33, 75
Benedictines, 51, 52, 53
Boulton, 119
"Bow-wow" hypothesis, 16
Bridgman, L., 40, 117
de Brosses, C., 15, 18
Buddhism, 65
Bulwer, J., 34, 75, 97

Cardano, J., 33
Chironomy, 99

Cicero, M. T., 96
Cistercians, 51, 52
Clark, W. P., 42, 43
Clerc, L., 35
Coleman, C., 67
Critchley, M., 29
— and Earl, C. J. C., 31
Cucurron, A., 33

Dactylology, 32, 33
Dance, 98–103
Darwin, C., 12, 117
Davis, T. K., 19, 21, 22, 23
Deaf-mutes, sign-language of, 28, 32–41, 103, 122
— aphasia in, 29
Definition of terms, 11
Dervishes, dancing, 112
Digitus medicus, 82
"Ding-dong" hypothesis, 16
Dix, Dom G., 75
Dubois, L., 52
Dumas, G., 12

Earl, C. J. C. and Critchley, M., 31
Efron, D. and Foley, J. P., 91, 92, 93
Eleusinian mysteries, 80
Elworthy, F. T., 78
De l'Epée, Abbé, 33, 35, 36
Epiloiacs, gesture in, 31
Expressive movements, exaggeration of, 30
— anatomical basis, 30

Fin, La, 33, 34
Foley, J. P. and Efron, D., 91, 92, 93
De Fontenay, S., 33

Gallaudet, T. H., 35, 40
De Gembloux, P., 119
Gillen, 48
Gogarty, O. St. J., 22
Goldstein, K., 26
Goldziher, I., 75
Grasset, 29
Gumilla, Fr., 76

Hadley, L. F., 43
Haga, C., 31
Hamilton, 28
Hatim's Tales, 61-2
Herrgot, the Abbé, 51
Hiero, 88
Hinduism, 65
Howitt, A. W., 48
Hung Society, 56, 57, 58

Immigrants, gesture in, 13, 92, 93
Infants, speech in, 120
Instinctive types of gesture, 36, 37, 38, 39, 40, 116, 117

Jackson, Hughlings, 11, 28
Jacovleff, A. and Tchou-Kia-Kien, 114
James, 75
Jespersen, O., 19, 21
De Jorio, Canon, 89, 90

Kagura, 112
Keller, H., 35

Kesson, J., 56
King, C. W., 54
De Kleen, T., 70, 71, 72
Knight, R. P., 54, 81
Krachininnikow, 76

Learned, 22, 119
Leibnitz, G. G., 51, 112
Lemoine, J. G., 75
Levantines, gesture among, 85-93
Lhermitte, J., 9
Lin Yutang, 115
Lloyd, A., 54
Long, S. H., 43
Lucian, 99, 107, 108
Lucretius, T., 15
Lutz, H. F., 78, 91

Mallery, G., 43, 44, 45, 122
Mano in fica, 82
Mano pantea, 81
Mantric signs, 83
Mantzius, K., 98
Manu cornuta, 81
Manus obscaena, 82
Maternus, J. F., 54
Martius, 76
Mawer, I., 100, 115
Mental defectives, speech in, 121
Miming, art of, 98
Montaigne, 35, 85, 118
Moor, A. P., 65
Moor, E., 65
Morlaas, J., 19
Mudra, 68, 69, 70, 71
Müller, M., 16, 18
Mythology, 65

INDEX

Nankikésvara, 111
Natural theories of language, 15
Natural types of gesture, 36, 37, 38, 39, 40, 116, 117
Nātya, 110
Neapolitans, gesture among, 85–93
Newman, Cardinal, 89, 90
"New Sign Language," 123
Nō plays, 112
North American Indians, sign-language among, 42–5

Ogden, C. K., 123
Onomatopoea, 16, 17, 18
Oriental literature, 59–64
Oseretsky, 13

Paget, Sir R., 19, 20, 21, 38, 49, 50, 123
Payne, A. H., 37
Penzer, N. M., 60, 61
Pereira, 33
Ponce de Leon, P., 33
"Pooh-pooh" hypothesis, 18

Quintilian, 86, 87, 94, 95, 96

Religious Communities, sign-language among, 51
Rhetoric, art of, 94–7
Roth, W. E., 46, 47
Rothman and Teuber, 23
Rossellius, 51
Rosa, L. A., 88

St. John of Beverley, 33
Schematopoea, 21

Schizophrenics, gesture in, 31
Schuchardt, 120
Schwidetzky, 119
Secret societies, sign-language among, 54
Seton, E. Thompson, 43, 74
Sibscota, 32
Sicard, Abbé, 35
Sicilians, gesture among, 88
Society of Brothers and Elders, 56, 57, 58
Society of Heaven and Earth, 56, 57, 58
Speech, in animals, 118, 119, 120
— in infants, 120
— in mental defectives, 120
Stirling, W. G. and Ward, J. S. M., 56
Swedenborg, 121
Symbolism, 78–84

Tawney, 59
Tschou-Kia-Kien and Jacovleff, A., 114
Teuber and Rothman, 23
Theatre, Chinese, 113, 114, 115
— Greek, 104, 105
— Indian, 110, 111, 112
— Japanese, 112
— Roman, 106, 107, 108, 109
Tictac system, 73, 74
Tomkins, W., 43
Tomlin, 56
Tooke, H., 18
Trappists, 51, 52, 53
Triad Society 56, 57, 58
Trumbull. 40
Tylor, E. B., 16, 17, 18, 23, 75

Vasomotor gestures, 31
Vernon, P. E. and Allport,
G. W., 14

Walpole, Hon. F. T., 54
Ward, J. S. M., 83
— and Stirling, W. G., 56

Wedgwood, H., 15
Westerman, 24
Wilkins, Bishop, 34, 74

Yerkes, 22
"Yo-heave-ho" hypothesis, 20

Zung, C. S. L., 114